WINNING
TOOLS

WINNING TOOLS

3 LEADERSHIP PRINCIPLES THAT BUILD **PURPOSE, RESPECT & SUCCESS**

MATTHEW MITCHELL

LIONCREST
PUBLISHING

COPYRIGHT © 2023 MATTHEW MITCHELL

WINNING TOOLS
3 Leadership Principles That Build Purpose, Respect & Success

ISBN 978-1-5445-4072-6 *Hardcover*

978-1-5445-4071-9 *Paperback*

978-1-5445-4070-2 *Ebook*

978-1-5445-4073-3 *Audiobook*

This book is dedicated to my parents,
John and Carol Mitchell.

They taught me the value of the Winning Tools.

Contents

Foreword

By: John C. Maxwell

THERE ARE NO SHORTCUTS TO ANY PLACE WORTHWHILE in life, no quick and easy roads to achievement. There are no accidental success stories. I've never met a person who made it to the top of the mountain and looked around, confused about how they got there. Winners are intentional. Greatness is always earned on difficult ground.

The first time I met Matthew Mitchell, I knew he was special. His resume speaks for itself: the all-time winningest women's coach at the University of Kentucky, three SEC Coach of the Year awards, and nine NCAA Tournament appearances, including three Elite Eight appearances. But he's more than successful. He's a person of substance. Behind all the accolades and honors is a strong, courageous leader who has built his life on great fundamentals, on the values he lives and teaches.

I admire great coaches. I grew up in Ohio playing basketball. I spent countless hours shooting baskets and working on my mechanics. I loved playing on a team and winning. Some of my earliest lessons about teamwork and leadership came on the basketball court under the direction of good coaches. But there's one thing I learned from an early age: you must master the fundamentals. If you lack the fundamentals when the big game arrives, your dreams of winning slip away from you. As my mentor John Wooden said, "When opportunity comes, it's too late to prepare." That's why coaches like my good friend Matthew Mitchell focus on the fundamentals.

The secret of your success is determined by your daily agenda. What you do is based on your principles and values. As you begin to read and study *Winning Tools*, you'll find values and principles that will help guide your thinking and actions when you develop them every day: honesty, hard work, and discipline. These are the fundamentals you must possess to step into your dream and make it a reality. The more consistent you are in focusing on these tools, the more consistently you will perform, and the greater the impact on your life and the lives of those around you.

We teach what we know, but we reproduce who we are. Matthew Mitchell is not just teaching what he knows in this book; he's reproducing who he is: a person of value who values people and adds value to them. Learn the lessons of *Winning Tools*. Embrace them. Live them. And you will not only climb mountains and achieve dreams; you will become a better person in the process.

Introduction

EVERYONE WAS PREDICTING ANOTHER SEASON OF MEDI-ocrity for my team. If that happened, I knew it might cost me my job.

The 2009–2010 basketball season was upcoming, and I was the head coach of the University of Kentucky's women's team. I'd been the coach at Kentucky for two years, and so far I had an uninspiring 33–32 overall record with zero NCAA tournament appearances.

No one was anticipating anything special for the coming season either. Not only was there no buzz of excitement, but most people thought we'd finish near the bottom of the standings. At that time, there were twelve teams in the Southeastern Conference (SEC), and the preseason poll predicted a tenth-place finish for us.

I was frustrated. Prior to the University of Kentucky, I had been the head coach at Morehead State. At Morehead, the program had won five games the season before I arrived. In my first season, we won sixteen games.

A turnaround at any program is challenging, and an eleven-win improvement felt great. This was the kind of fast impact I had hoped for at Kentucky.

Morehead State was a smaller program that played in the Ohio Valley Conference (OVC), and the circumstances at Kentucky were different. It's no knock on Morehead State to say that Kentucky came with more pressure and expectations.

It's just reality that when you are in the SEC, programs have more resources. And that means they can afford to make coaching changes faster when winning doesn't happen as quickly as everyone would like. It is also a more competitive landscape for recruiting. Everything is ratcheted up a notch.

I needed time to adjust to all that, and maybe you could argue that explained my team's overall record through two seasons. But I wasn't in the mood for making excuses. For one, I don't like excuses. For two, nobody wanted to listen or would've cared. This is big-time college sports where you either get the job done or you won't be the head coach for very long. It's exceptionally competitive with high expectations, as it should be.

If the preseason predictions for a tenth-place finish came true, I might get fired. At a minimum, it would certainly put me on the "hot seat," and the pressure would get even more intense. More importantly, job considerations aside, I wanted to win. Not just for me, but for my dedicated staff, for the young women that played for me, and for the university community and our great fans.

With the pressure I was feeling both internally and externally, I knew something needed to change, but I couldn't quite put my finger on it. At Morehead State, I had come up with what I called the Winning Tools: Honesty, Hard Work, and Discipline. These three character-based concepts formed the basis of the culture I built at Morehead State, and I was using the same tools at Kentucky.

I knew that many good college coaches had their own tools and concepts that they used as the guiding lights to build winning programs. Pat Summit, the legendary coach at the University of Tennessee, had her Definite Dozen.

I loved the idea of having clear values that could anchor an entire program and create a winning culture. But I also didn't want to simply copy someone else. I thought long and hard about what creates success and then distilled it down to its essence and came up with the three tools that could work in any area of life.

The fact that there were only three tools was important. Three was simple enough to keep centered on what mattered. But each of the three was also powerful enough to lay the foundation for great success.

Still, something was a little off at Kentucky. My mediocre record told me that, and my gut was telling me the same thing. I was preaching the 3 Winning Tools to my assistant coaches and my players, and I was trying to live them out as a coach and a human being. I knew the tools were solid. What was wrong?

I decided I needed to go deep with the first tool and be totally and radically honest with myself. When I did, I realized that I was trying to be someone else, to build my program on someone else's ideal. The royalty in the SEC at the time was Coach Summit and her Tennessee Lady Vols.

Coach Summit was an excellent recruiter and looked for the biggest and toughest at every position. And she usually got them. Because of that, her teams were strong, physical, and very hard to beat at their own game. If you were going to pick a program to emulate at that time, it was the gold standard.

But it was still a mistake. I wasn't going to beat Tennessee at their own game, and I wasn't going to out-recruit Coach Summit for the kind of player she wanted for her teams. In looking honestly at the players I did have, I realized we weren't the biggest and the baddest, and nothing was going to change that.

However, once I stopped trying to force my team into the wrong mold, I realized something else. What we were was fast and athletic. I needed to go back to the drawing board, adjust my game plan, and give my players the best possible chance to compete and win using the gifts and skills they did have.

I also rededicated myself to being a better leader in exemplifying and teaching the 3 Tools. I decided to stop worrying about how many wins we would get or my own job status. The focus would be on doing things the right way, with Honesty, Hard Work, and Discipline. From there, the results would either come or they wouldn't.

No shortcuts. No hand-wringing about what our record would be. No obsessing on my own job status. I owed my team that, I owed my coaches that, and I owed myself that.

The overlap between sports and business is fascinating. It's why you so often hear sports metaphors used in the business world. They're both competitive arenas, where you have to produce results or your job is at risk. They both require excellent leaders who can build the best teams and motivate top performance.

- I've found that upper management executives and CEOs can fall into the exact same traps that I was tripping over in my early tenure at Kentucky:

- Instead of keeping the concentration on your own team and its strengths, you start to get too caught up on what your competitors are doing

- The pressure for results tempts you to look for short-cuts instead of relying on a character-based culture that lays the foundation for long-term success

- Sometimes you worry too much about your own status and security instead of being a truly selfless leader who focuses on serving your team

Coaching and business leadership also both require solving day-to-day problems, including responding to those inevitable surprises and changing market conditions that often call for quick and decisive action.

What great leaders need are a fundamental set of tools that can guide both long-term strategy and day-to-day needs. Tools that work for every level of the organization and can create a winning culture and a healthy team.

THE 3 WINNING TOOLS

This book is dedicated to explaining the 3 Tools, and why and how they work. Just as importantly, it will show how you can implement them as a business leader.

Tool #1: Honesty

If you simply think of honesty as telling the bare minimum truth, that's not a winning tool. The kind of honesty I'm talking about means surfacing all the issues, always acting with integrity, and being truthful with yourself about how much effort you're putting forth.

It's crucial that this tool comes first. It's the foundation of everything you and your team do because you can't truly solve problems if you're not being real about them. Sometimes using this tool will hurt, but that means you're doing it right.

Tool #2: Hard Work

Here's another simple-sounding tool that has deeper layers. To be a good leader, you need to help your team get a clear understanding of the value of hard work and how it can transform organizations (and also lives). People are willing to work harder once they understand its value.

You also need to make sure that you and your team are working hard at the right things. There's nothing more frustrating than pouring significant effort into the wrong things, but it happens all the time in business.

Hard work also requires mental toughness if you want to sustain it. You need to know how to challenge team members to overcome obstacles, but also when they need positive inspiration.

Tool #3: Discipline

The first two tools will lead you to the third. Discipline is the glue that will keep you being honest and working hard. I'll share strategies for implementing discipline into your leadership, the kind of discipline that can sustain long-term success.

Discipline relies heavily on mental toughness. How do you keep the right attitude, even when things seem to be going against you? And do you often overreact in the moment, or are you developing the skill of perspective? As a leader, if you fail at discipline, so will your team.

WHY I'M WRITING THIS BOOK

There's a lot of pressure on business leaders today. If you're in a middle- to upper-management position, getting to the next level is hard. (Sometimes even maintaining your position is challenging!) It's easy to get lost in the day-to-day struggles and lose the forest for the trees.

What leaders need is a clear set of guiding principles and a way to implement them. When I retired from basketball coaching,

I saw how the Winning Tools could serve any aspiring business leader by keeping them focused on what really matters. Getting to the highest levels of leadership requires a commitment to fundamentals that will work in every situation.

So the book you're holding in your hands is for those who aim to go higher and get to the top. It's also for CEOs and others already there who want to create a culture that gets amazing results in any business climate.

Along the way, I'll tell you some stories from my life and coaching career that I hope you'll find fun and entertaining, but also useful. Please don't just read this book and say, "Well, those tools sound like a pretty nice thing," and then close it and never make a serious effort to implement them in your life and your business leadership.

That would be a shame because if you seriously commit to leading with the Winning Tools, the results are extraordinary. Using the tools of Honesty, Hard Work, and Discipline can make the difference between a stagnant career and one that goes to the next level. These tools will empower everyone on your team and help create the kind of guiding purpose that only the greatest companies achieve.

I also don't want you to think you will ever be done with the Winning Tools. It's not like you will reach a point where you say, "Okay, I've mastered the tools, my leadership skills are set, and it will be smooth sailing from here on out."

That would be great, but you know it is not realistic. Even after years of practicing and developing the Winning Tools, I still fall short sometimes. There have been times—even recently—when I became blind to mistakes I was making. In those situations, I needed a friend or mentor to say, "Coach, you need to take a look at yourself in this area."

If you are an aspiring business leader, or are already in a leadership position, you probably know exactly what I am talking about. We all have those painful moments of insight when we suddenly recognize that our actions don't match our ideals.

Here's the wonderful thing about the Winning Tools. They work in these situations too. They are structured to help you get back on track. When you find an area of your life, your career, or your leadership that is out of alignment with your values, you return to the Winning Tools to get back on the path of success. The Honesty tool forces you to candidly assess what is really happening. Once you know the way back, Hard Work and Discipline will help you close the gap.

Then you will no doubt make other mistakes, but hopefully each time you learn something and become a better leader. The Winning Tools will be your lifelong success formula if you sincerely work at them.

THE SECRET BEHIND THE TOOLS

What is the secret to the power of the Tools, and why do they work so well? I believe the key is that each tool is rooted in principle-based thinking. It is so easy to start making decisions based on emotion or to give in to some external pressure. It's also too easy to become so focused on the result that you are tempted by shortcuts.

With the right principles to guide your thinking and actions, you avoid these traps. And what is amazing is what happens in your life and your career when you sincerely implement the Winning Tools. You become a more purposeful person, and one who can sustain a commitment to your purpose. You earn more respect from those around you because they can sense your integrity. And it all comes together in levels of success you didn't know were possible.

I should probably tell you what happened in that third season at Kentucky after I stopped trying to copy someone else's success and rededicated myself and my team to the Winning Tools.

We finished second in the SEC instead of the predicted tenth. Our record ended up being 28–8 (after being 16–16 the previous year). We not only made the NCAA tournament, we went all the way to the Elite Eight. We swept the SEC postseason awards with the Player of the Year, the Freshman of the Year, and the Coach of the Year. It was a remarkable season!

The credit for all this, of course, goes well beyond me. The players took the tools to heart and earned the wins on the court. That's one of the things that makes the Winning Tools so valuable: people respond to them and are inspired. Once someone understands the power of these simple but incredibly effective concepts, they climb aboard. Honesty, Hard Work, and Discipline work everywhere, on the court and off, in business, at home, and in life.

They also bring lasting success. From that season until my retirement in 2020, our team won more than twenty games in every season but one. We went to the NCAA tournament eight more times, including two more trips to the Elite Eight, and two trips to the Sweet Sixteen.

The 3 Winning Tools are for leaders who are committed to this kind of sustained success. Invest in them as both an individual and a leader, and you'll be amazed by what you accomplish. The best place to start is with the Honesty tool, to which we now turn.

PART ONE

WINNING TOOL #1

Honesty

1

Honesty

ALMOST EVERYONE WAS ENCOURAGING ME TO LIE.

I was still a young man at this point, a high school basketball coach lucky enough to be invited to be a part of a summer camp run by Pat Summit, the legendary coach at the University of Tennessee.

This was the summer of 1996, and participation at her summer camp was exploding. Coach Summit had become one of the biggest names in all of women's sports because of her phenomenal record as a coach. Her reputation was well deserved, and she had just won her fourth national championship (she would go on to rack up a total of eight NCAA Championships).

With this outstanding reputation, she had attracted over one thousand kids from all over the country to come to her camp. There were one hundred coaches on staff, and I was one of them. Each of us was assigned ten campers that we were responsible for.

At the initial meeting of all the coaches and camp counselors, Coach Summit had emphasized one point in particular: "The number one rule is don't be late. You cannot be late. If you're late, you're fired."

That was literally her line—"if you're late, you're fired"—and this was repeated to us by others until it was burned into our brains.

That might sound like a terribly harsh punishment, but it actually made a lot of sense. With one thousand kids and all the responsibility that entailed, you had to have rules like this or you would have chaos.

So, guess who was late to meet his campers two days later?

Yes, that's right.

ME.

We had a break for lunch, and I went back to my dorm room. About thirty minutes before we were supposed to return, some of the other coaches in my dorm invited me to walk back with them. "No, we still have some time," I told them. "I'll come in a few minutes."

I was enjoying a book I was reading, and the air conditioning felt great. So why not enjoy it for a few more minutes, right?

And then I fell asleep. Right there, in the chair, sound asleep!

When I woke up, the clock showed I was already ten minutes late. I immediately freaked out, racing down the stairs and then into a full sprint across campus. I cannot recall the actual distance, but it sure felt like a mile in the moment.

In the meantime, roll call had already happened, and my name had gotten out through the walkie-talkies used at the camp. "Matthew Mitchell's late. Who's Matthew Mitchell? I don't know who this guy is. He is brand new."

I finally arrived, and all the other coaches in my group are just looking at me wide-eyed. They're staring at me with a mixture of pity and alarm that only confirmed for me that I was in big trouble. If I had any notion that I was exaggerating in my mind how much hot water I was in, I knew from their looks that I was truly in for it. I remember I kept thinking over and over, *This is the worst thing ever.*

And that's when a few of the younger coaches started to encourage me to lie. The consensus among that group was that my best shot was to say I wasn't feeling well. That seemed like the most reasonable excuse for being delayed. Not much you can do about getting sick, right?

I felt my inner resolve weakening, and I was starting to lean toward telling the lie. Getting this job at this point in my life had been important to me. A friend of mine, Kim Rosamond, was a player at the University of Mississippi at the time and was a counselor at this camp and had helped me get this opportunity. (Coach Rosamond would later go on to become an outstanding head coach at Tennessee Tech).

I knew I could learn a lot here and also network with some experienced coaches, which was invaluable. The $250 a week stipend was also something that came in handy at that time in my life.

Here I was about to throw this opportunity away. My options weren't great. Tell the truth and certainly get fired. Tell a lie and improve my chances of keeping my job.

The decision to claim I was sick would feel awful. But then again, getting fired like this would have been humiliating. Being fired from a summer camp anywhere would be bad, but getting fired by the greatest women's basketball coach of all time? Who would want Pat Summit to think they were an irresponsible fool, yell at them, and then get booted from her camp? Lying started to sound like a viable option.

As I thought about it, someone spoke up with authority. It was Pat Gray, a great person and a terrific coach. At the time she was a high school coach in Alabama and was well respected at the Lady Vols camp. She was the one in charge of our group of coaches.

"You tell the truth, and then you just accept whatever comes," Coach Gray told me. "She's a fair woman. Don't go to her making up stories."

What Coach Gray did in that moment was remind me of what my parents had worked so hard to instill in me: be honest. Not kind of honest. Not honest only when it is convenient. Just. Be. Honest.

I'm still not sure to this day if I would have stood strong to the principle of honesty if Coach Gray hadn't reminded me of the values I was raised on. My decision was made. I would tell the truth. I'll tell you about what happened next a little later in this chapter.

There's a reason honesty is the *first* Winning Tool. You cannot make any real progress without it, not as an individual and not as a leader.

Of course, sometimes a lie (or something less than the truth) will have a short-term benefit, or at least feel like it does. But if you truly want long-term, lasting success for yourself and your organization, honesty is the most important fundamental.

Here's the thing about the word "honesty." There is sometimes a tendency to talk about it as if it was only about ethics. It's good for you, but doesn't taste that great, like eating spinach when you're a kid. You do it because "it's the right thing."

I completely agree that it is the right thing to do, and you should do it even when it hurts. That is character, which is the foundation of leadership. But the benefits of honesty go beyond morality, and that is important to remember.

You cannot expect to solve problems or make improvements to your business and your life if you do not have a firm and truthful grasp of where you truly stand at the moment. The same goes for communication with those you work with. A healthy organization must be rooted in honesty.

As a coach, it didn't do my players any good if I tried to dance around a player's weaknesses when talking to them (of course, that doesn't mean you should be rude, angry, or intimidating either—more on that later in the book). This same principle applies for business leaders. For example, it doesn't do you any good to be less than honest in delivering a performance appraisal just to avoid hurt feelings or awkward conversations.

Honesty goes all the way down to the most basic level. In basketball, you review tape over and over to find out the facts about your opponents. Without an accurate assessment, there is no way to create a successful game plan. It would be as if your company had a profit and loss statement filled with wrong information. There would be absolutely no way to make any sense of anything.

We all understand this at some level. As I will point out in several places in this book, the Winning Tools are simple. But as I also point out, *simple is NOT the same as easy*. Almost everyone will immediately agree that honesty matters, and you have to know where you are to figure out where to go next. But we need to do more than quickly agree; we need to truly reflect on the importance of honesty and how hard it can sometimes be to stick with this tool when you are under pressure.

Without a consistent, bedrock commitment to honesty, it is impossible to make real, sustained progress. You must know where you are in order to know how to get where you want to go.

Now let's dig a little deeper into ways to bring more honesty into your business life.

OBSESSING ABOUT RESULTS CAN LEAD TO SHORTCUTS

You may recall from the book's introduction that when I was struggling at the University of Kentucky, one of the conclusions I came to was that I was getting too wrapped up in worrying about winning and about job security.

Don't get me wrong; no matter what your career is, winning and holding onto your job are almost always good things. But if you focus too much on the results (winning, reaping huge profits, being honored, etc.), you can hurt your chances of getting all those things.

What do I mean by that? If you focus on "the ends"—what you want to get or accomplish—then you get tempted to let the ends "justify the means." Shortcuts begin to look more attractive. Sometimes they even work in the short term. But they fail as a long-term strategy.

During my third season at Kentucky, when my team and I recommitted to building a culture based on strong character first, the wins followed. We were honest, we worked hard, and we were disciplined. That's what we focused on, not obsessing about wins and losses. And it was then that the wins happened.

DEFINING RIGOROUS HONESTY

Whenever I coach business leaders about this tool, I like to refer to this tool as not just honesty, but as *rigorous* honesty. I believe this concept is the touchstone of every truly successful leader. It's the secret sauce that's going to take you from good to great.

The rigorous part comes from taking honesty several steps further than minimum truth-telling. Most people understand from the time they are children that it's important not to lie. When I started thinking about how I was going to focus on honesty in my life and with my team, I realized it wasn't going to be enough to just meet the barest standard of "not lying."

To rise higher than where we were at the moment, and to exceed ordinary achievement, requires extraordinary standards. It means digging deeper, being vigorous in our efforts to be completely honest with ourselves and with each other.

Rigorous honesty, when embraced completely, goes beyond simple truth telling. Rigorous honesty requires stripping away the "sugar" we use to sweeten hard truths, eliminating excuses, dealing solely with the facts, and most importantly, holding everyone accountable for their actions and choices. This type of honesty, when implemented daily, will reshape an organization's culture and build a solid foundation for success.

If you've ever tried to slant or spin a story to get yourself out of trouble, you already know the difference between rigorous honesty versus just making something up that is based on a true story. It's certainly possible to tell the truth without telling the WHOLE truth in order to make yourself look better.

Rigorous honesty is a two-way street. You cannot expect honesty from others, especially anyone that reports to you, if you are not honest with them. You may need to tell them that the current marketing strategy—the one they created and that you approved—is losing money. You might have to share unpleasant economic realities the company is facing and what the consequences of that may be in the long term.

If employees or members of your team get the feeling that transparency only goes one way, you can't build a culture of honesty. Related to this is the ability to not just encourage feedback, but also to actually hear it. The natural, unthinking reaction to a perspective that doesn't match ours is to immediately start trying to find ways to reject it. Commit instead to listen carefully to what is being said and truly hear and consider whether change is necessary.

The most important thing to understand when starting on a journey of rigorous honesty is that it's not going to be easy. Many times over the years I've caught myself being less rigorously honest than I should have been when talking to my team or my players. I was afraid that what I had to say would hurt them. I would tell myself that whoever I was talking to couldn't handle the truth, so I would tidy up the message in my mind to make it more palatable for them.

Sugarcoating a message so that it's easier for a person to hear might make it easier for me to deal with their reaction in the short term, but the reality is that I'm not doing either of us any favors. Over time, I learned that being completely honest with my team required me to lay out the facts in as straightforward a manner as possible and let the chips fall where they may.

Rigorous honesty doesn't end with others, however. It also means being honest with yourself, and as I know too well, there are times when that's considerably more difficult than being honest with someone else. If you can begin to master this type of stringent self-honesty, it is actually very motivating. Eliminating the option to make an excuse or manipulate the facts to let yourself off the hook gives you the kind of honest feedback that will allow you to improve.

As these small improvements begin to snowball, you become more and more successful and then more and more motivated. Once you recognize the behaviors that hold you back and understand the actions that move you forward, your ability to follow through and produce excellent results will skyrocket.

There were many situations throughout my coaching career where I had to dig deep to push past my own ego and fully integrate rigorous honesty into my work, but it was worth it every single time.

BRINGING RIGOROUS HONESTY TO YOUR WHOLE LIFE

Who you are in one part of your life will impact every other part of your life. We sometimes tend to think we can wall off our work life from our family life from our time with friends, without one area impacting another.

You might be able to maintain some kind of artificial wall between your personal, family, and business lives for a time, but the character you build overall will eventually influence every area of your life. Tell lies at home, and you will eventually find it easier to lie at work.

So you need to own up to your spouse that you forgot to pick up the dry cleaning instead of saying it wasn't ready when you stopped by. You need to sit down with your child and be honest about their less-than-acceptable effort with their schoolwork and why it matters.

It is crucial to also be honest about the good things, too, something we often forget. Have you told your spouse how much you appreciate them taking over all the kid duties when you had to travel a lot last month? Did you sit that same child down and tell them you have noticed how much their math grade has improved since they began putting in extra time on their schoolwork every night?

Building up your rigorous honesty muscles anywhere will make it easier to use them everywhere.

Remember to use this honest praise in a work setting too. Make a point of telling your marketing manager that they made a great choice with that unconventional strategy that many people said would fail.

Good or bad, rigorous honesty takes the ego out of the equation and deals with the facts. It's not designed to be purposefully brutal, or to deliberately hurt other people, but it requires that we not be incomplete with the truth.

In the next chapter, we will go even deeper into this topic, but first let me tell you what happened to the young version of myself all those years ago at Pat Summit's camp.

As you recall, I had managed to be late at the camp where the mantra was, "If you're late, you're fired." And I had already made my decision to tell the truth. But then I had to get through my afternoon coaching session before I would go face the music with Coach Summit. It gave me plenty of time to be nervous, which I was.

When I went to see her, there was a line of people ahead of me to talk with her. With a camp that big, she always had someone that needed to talk to her. Finally, I reached the head of the line.

"Coach Summit, I'm Matthew Mitchell."

"Oh, I've heard about you," she said. "I know who you are. What's going on here?"

She was an intense person, and now she knew who I was for all the wrong reasons. It was very intimidating having her ask me sharply what was going on.

I took a deep breath and plunged ahead. "It was after lunch. I was reading in my dorm and I fell asleep. I'm sorry. I don't have a good excuse, it was irresponsible, and I apologize."

There was a pause that felt like an eternity. She eyed me closely, seeming to weigh me on some kind of scale. And then she said, "Don't let it happen again. We're going to be keeping an eye on you, and you better not be late again."

And with that, I had received absolution.

The reaction from others was as if a minor miracle had occurred. I would return for several more camps over the next few years, moving up in the ranks and becoming better known for better reasons. I also became part of the camp lore, known as "Matthew Mitchell, the only person to ever survive being late at Pat Summit's camp."

Amazingly, several years later I would work for Coach Summit, getting a coveted assistant's job at the University of Tennessee. She would sometimes tease me a little bit about granting me a second chance. But she also told me something that made me understand I really had come very close to getting fired. She apparently had decided in the moment to grant me a reprieve.

"A feeling came over me at the time, in listening to you, that I needed to give you another chance," was how she described it.

Call it luck, call it a reward for choosing honesty, or just say I caught one of the best coaches ever at a moment of grace. Over the next few years, that camp would give me the opportunity to grow and show my energy and enthusiasm and that I wasn't afraid to work hard. That camp led to many good things for me and gave me relationships I cherish to this day.

And you better believe I made sure I was never late to any camp event or session ever again.

2

Integrity

HAVING A FRIEND AND MENTOR WILLING TO HOLD UP A mirror to you and tell you the truth is one of the most valuable things in the world.

It can also hurt like heck.

I was reminded of this from a conversation I had several years back with a truly remarkable assistant coach I had at Kentucky, Lin Dunn. Coach Dunn has accomplished so much in her career, including a WNBA Championship as head coach of the Indiana Fever, and a place in the Women's Basketball Hall of Fame.

She had essentially retired from coaching basketball, but then unretired to help me. It was an amazing honor for me to have someone of this experience and reputation on staff at Kentucky.

But now she was sitting across the table from me telling me something I did not want to hear. Her message boiled down to this: I was too angry, and it was impacting my players and the program in a negative way.

Ouch.

If it had been almost anyone but Coach Dunn, I think I would have tried to find ways to deflect this. I felt defensiveness welling up inside me. I wanted to rationalize, dismiss, or at least minimize the behavior she was pointing out.

To understand the full context, this was many years into my tenure as a head coach at Kentucky. We had some wonderful success over the last several years. So maybe sometimes I did get a little too angry and really let the players or a referee have it. But you can't make an omelet without breaking a few eggs, right? The proof was there in the wins and losses, and even if I wasn't always perfect, I was getting the job done.

Those are all the things I *wanted* to tell myself. But no, lying to myself would not work. For one thing, the woman sitting across from me had way too much integrity and good judgment for me to brush off what she was saying.

32

There were also the plain facts if I could bring myself to look at them with fresh, clear eyes. I relied on sarcasm to motivate players. I would raise my voice in anger when things did not go the way I wanted. I would go overboard with intensity toward the players if I thought it would help get my point across.

I had to admit it to myself. I would try to dominate players with anger, and I used fear to push players to improve their performance. This was a perfectly accepted way of coaching as I was growing up, and I think it still influences coaching and leadership to this day. (I'll discuss this aspect of coaching and leadership in more depth in Chapter 9.)

Anger and fear were not the only way I motivated players, and I truly did care for them. But still, I had to acknowledge that I had convinced myself that it was okay to get angry if I thought it helped my players get better and drove them to achieve more. It was dawning on me now that I did not have a lot of control when I was in a rage. This was not a great motivating tool I was using skillfully; it was a blunt instrument doing more harm than good.

And that was just with my players. That paled in comparison to how angry I would get with the referees.

I had at least made a commitment to myself that I would not curse at them. Other coaches were cursing them, but I wasn't doing that, so I thought that must have meant I was treating them alright.

The problem with this no cursing rule was that it allowed me to tell myself that anything else I did was just fine. I would yell, scream, and gesture wildly. Sometimes it was just a complete loss of composure.

It was one such incident that was the final straw for Coach Dunn, and she knew it was time to talk. We had had a game the night before in Missouri, and I totally lost it on the officials. The next day she told me: "When you get like that, you are not focused on coaching the team. You are more focused on yelling at the officials. It's not good for you. It's not good for your coaches. And it's definitely not good for your players."

Coach Dunn used the word "hijacked" in the conversation, and that is how I came to think of what happened to me when I got too angry. My mind lost total focus and was given over completely to my anger; my mind was hijacked in these situations and could no longer be put in service to helping my team.

Up to that point, I had been justifying angry tirades at the officials as "sticking up for my team." But looking at it in the cold light of day with Coach Dunn, I knew that I wasn't helping the team at all when I let my mind be hijacked with rage.

As the conversation continued, we discussed how this anger problem went deeper than referees. All the things I mentioned above about how I sometimes dealt with players started to become clearer to me. I had a problem, and it had to be addressed.

All of these things are a little hard and embarrassing to admit, even though I've made great strides in this area, something I will share more about later.

But since this is a book about character-based leadership, I think it is worth sharing this story even though it kind of hurts to do it. It illustrates some hugely important lessons. One lesson is that success does not shield you from counter-productive behaviors. If you think that success equals "I must be doing everything right," this story says otherwise. I was the winningest coach in the University of Kentucky's women's basketball, and here I was setting this example of anger and sometimes even mind-hijacking rage.

This story also shows that self-deception is relatively easy. If you want to rationalize a behavior, you can almost always find a way.

But the most important lesson for this chapter is that whatever mistakes you are making, your sense of integrity is what can save you.

Confronted by a person of integrity with real facts about my actual behavior, I had to face up to it. And what forced me to look at it squarely was my own sense of integrity. Preaching these character-based tools all the time, and then failing to be honest about my own need to change, would have been too big a contradiction.

This is hugely important for leaders. People can spot hypocrisy, and it will erode their faith that you can lead them. Mistakes and even massive flaws can be overcome, but you have to have the integrity to listen to others and admit when you must do the hard work of change.

BUILDING TRUST

Honesty and integrity must be the basis of the relationship you build with your team.

When I first started climbing the career ladder, I had this idea in my head that once I became the boss, I could do whatever I wanted, and people would just have to deal with it. I would have all the leeway.

I couldn't have been more wrong. What I actually discovered was that if I was going to say that honesty is important, when I got to the top of an organization, I had to be the one to live it out. There was no one above me telling me how to do things. Integrity was something that I would have to choose myself to model every day.

RESOLVING CONFLICT

A culture of honesty and integrity in an organization is crucial for resolving conflict. Every organization inevitably generates conflict, and you have to find ways to resolve it in a way that is productive instead of damaging. Over the course of my career, I've come to believe that most conflict is rooted in confusion about expectations.

Great leaders focus on clear and honest setting of expectations for their team, but they do not stop there. They also create the kind of environment where the team can communicate the expectations they have of the leader. It is this open, two-way street of honesty and integrity that is vital in building a positive leadership environment.

I always appreciated leaders who acted this way during my career. At the University of Kentucky, I always had a great relationship with the athletic director, Mitch Barnhart, and the university president, Dr. Eli Capilouto, and a big part of that was that they never beat around the bush when it came to telling me what was on their minds and what their expectations were. When facts and objectives are presented to me with total honesty, I use them as the guideposts to find a path forward to success.

Integrity in leadership also allows an organization to adapt to bad news or hard truths because they trust the person that the news is coming from. An example of this was the story I opened this chapter with. Coach Dunn knew she could approach me with a hard truth. Everyone could see the problem but me— you won't be fooling your team about your weaknesses. A culture of integrity allowed this communication to happen.

This kind of honesty will also help address specific business problems. Consider the company that's facing rapidly decreasing profits. There's going to need to be either a sharp change in strategy or multiple layoffs. At that point, leadership is faced with a choice.

You can hide the state of the company from your team and hope you can change course without looping them in, figuring it is better not to panic or discourage anyone. Bad choice, because it is likely to backfire.

These are the people that are front and center with your customers every single day. They know more about what happens day-to-day in your building than you do. Telling them everything is fine when it's not does not boost their confidence in the business situation; it's just going to erode their confidence in you.

On the other hand, being upfront and honest about your business affairs stabilizes your relationship with your team and sends the message that you trust them with key information. It also connects you to a wealth of experience and ideas to help your company course correct that you wouldn't have if you hid it from them. Integrity means speaking the facts as they are.

Some coaches deliberately suppress praise for a player to keep them motivated and drive them harder. Other coaches take a player who is in a slump and tell them everything is fine. Neither one of these tactics is in the best interest of the team; it erodes trust and makes it difficult for coaches to truly connect with and motivate their players. They can spot when you are not acting with integrity.

My philosophy as a coach and business leader has been to motivate my team with a commitment to deal with the situation in front of us. When you earn a reputation for dealing with the facts, your team learns to trust what you say. Taking the guesswork out of the relationship allows your team to shift their focus away from any mind games they think you may be playing and puts it back on their own performance.

Integrity also means having to hold people accountable to the rules of the organization without bias and even when it hurts. Especially when it hurts. During the 2015 NCAA tournament, we had an 11:00 p.m. curfew. Our senior starting center missed the curfew by a few minutes.

This left me in a tough spot. Players knew the consequences of missing curfew would be very severe, but I never said precisely what the penalty would be. This was intentional. Spelling out the exact consequences of infractions could lead players to make trade-off decisions about team rules. "Yes, I'll break that rule because I can handle that punishment, and I'd rather enjoy myself now."

Instead, I wanted players to follow the rules because it was the right thing to do for the team, and I did not want to tempt them into "trade-off" thinking.

I knew darn well that if this were the regular season, I would've no doubt suspended the curfew breaker for the entire next game. Doing it now would hurt more, given that we were in the NCAA tournament. But my gut told me that I should stick to the principle I would have upheld any other time, and so I suspended her for the game.

We were highly favored going into the game, and we ended up losing. Sometimes making a decision with integrity hurts in the short term. There was a lot of disappointment surrounding the loss at the time, but it was the right decision and benefited our long-term team integrity greatly.

FREEDOM TO MAKE RADICAL DECISIONS

One of my hallmarks as a coach was radical decision making. Translation: I was willing to buck tradition and choose a less popular path because I knew it was the right one for my team. I found that the willingness to make radical decisions was a key part of helping to turn around a team quickly at Morehead State and also to make changes in my third year at Kentucky.

I think what gives a leader the necessary confidence to go against the grain is the commitment to honesty, and then the integrity to follow through on a different plan. When you feel like you have a good grasp of the facts and have made an honest assessment of them, then you make the plan you think best fits the facts.

Honesty puts excellent leaders in a position to evaluate circumstances, identify goals, and focus on the problems that need to be solved to turn those goals into realities.

It sounds simpler than it often is in practice. Many of us keep going along with what everyone else is doing or stay on a present course because it feels safer and easier, and we have not dug enough into the facts.

I love this quote attributed to Aubrey De Graf: "Don't cling to a mistake just because you spent a lot of time making it." Honesty allowed me in the third season to see that I was trying to be successful like Tennessee (big, intimidating players overpowering you) instead of allowing my players to best use the talents they had (smaller but faster). Honesty and integrity allowed me to stop clinging to a mistake and instead let our strategy match the facts about our program.

Business leaders face these same challenges, of course. Time and money have been invested in a particular strategy, and the data starts coming back that shows it is not working. After rigorous analysis, it becomes clear that the strategy is failing. The fix is going to be costly, both in terms of embarrassment and in real costs.

Excellent leadership is willing to change the situation radically when the facts warrant it, paying the necessary emotional and financial cost. You can only do that if you are committed to integrity.

Being willing to make decisive reversals of bad hiring decisions is another area that will test your leadership ability. I
learned this lesson very painfully at one of my coaching jobs.

I brought someone on to my staff who was excellent in some
areas but had some red flags in others. Those red flags were
in areas that could cause interpersonal conflicts that could
impact team morale. Despite this, I hired the person, thinking I could monitor and change the negative behavior while
getting the benefits of this person's talents in other areas.

It did not work, but even worse, I did not have a firm grasp of
the amount of conflict that was being stirred up. By the time I
did have a fuller understanding, significant damage had been
done to the program. I not only had to part ways with this
assistant coach quickly, but I now had healing and rebuilding
to do.

Being willing to hire the person despite some reservations was
part of the mistake, but my real error was not being honest
with myself and my team about the conflicts. If I had, I could
have corrected my original mistake before it had a chance to
grow.

Our mistakes tend to keep growing when we do not have the
integrity to face up to them sooner. We then find out that the
deeper the hole we dig, the harder it will be to climb out of it.
This is what I discovered when Coach Dunn helped me see
that my anger was a problem.

Human nature being what it is, we prefer our solutions fast and simple. If something is easily solved, I certainly have nothing against it. But real problems, issues that we have ignored for years or even decades, cannot be wished away. You did not get into this in a day, and it is not going away in a day.

As I came to a fuller realization of how I had let anger get the best of me, it also became clear that I was not going to be able to change by telling myself, *Just don't get angry.* Habitual responses and ways we interact with others get ingrained deeply, and we do not always have the necessary knowledge on how to really change.

I decided to turn to a certified counselor with professional expertise on helping people to better channel emotional responses in less harmful and more productive ways. It was a journey!

For example—and this sounds kind of crazy to me now—I had convinced myself that the referees had it out for me because I was the new guy in the conference. They gave the calls to the experienced coaches in the league, the ones with the bigger reputations.

As the counselor helped me remove the lens that filtered facts through my emotions, I realized this was ridiculous. In the moment of making a call, did I really think the referee was consulting the color of the uniform before making it? They were going to make some mistakes and border-line calls, of course. But it was only my own response that created the notion that somehow the referees had it out for me. That is a textbook case of not dealing with the facts honestly.

This counseling helped me also face up to my use of anger to motivate players. When I had a chance to see this from a distance, it became clear to me that this contradicted many of the other things I said to my team about how we treat others. I also had the key insight that anger is not the effective technique that many coaches think it is. Being sarcastic and dismissive is not nearly as good as being firm and clear on what you do want your players to do. I'll share more about how to do that in Chapter 9.

If I had been honest with myself, I would have recognized that I was belittling them, even though that wasn't my intention. I was modeling a behavior that created an environment that was the exact opposite of the culture I wanted to create, and in doing so, I built resentment between myself, my coaching staff, and my team.

I got away with this in my own head because at heart, I'm a pretty warm, fun-loving guy. I really did want the best for my players. But your good qualities do not cancel out your bad ones, at least not if you want to live with integrity.

Today, I am still not perfect, of course, but I have to say that the counseling gave me the tools to change. I also read books on anger management, and I did a lot of soul searching. It is a choice I make every day to live differently, and my life is much better for it.

3

Honest Effort

I WON THE PARENT LOTTERY.

Winning the parent lottery has nothing to do with money or worldly status. I'm sure all of us know people raised with every material advantage and with total financial security who turned out very unhappy and ethically challenged.

It also has nothing to do with looks or athletic skills or even being a genius. All those things are fine, but that's not the greatest gift parents can give their children.

Winning the parent lottery means being raised to be a person who is honest and works hard and does not bend whichever way the wind is blowing. And great parents do not just talk about it; they model it.

My parents were very clear with me and my brothers from a very young age that going down the road to dishonesty was something you had to stop before it even got started. Taking even one step down that road makes it easier to take the next step. You need to tell more lies and continue omitting other truths to cover up that first step. It was ingrained in us that honesty was the expectation.

An incident from when I was fourteen years old impressed this upon me in a deeper way. I grew up in Mississippi, and at the time, you could get your driver's license at fifteen. I happened to be the youngest of my friends, and so the last to drive. My friends were going out and having weekend adventures and I wanted in on it.

The problem was my parents were adamant that you had to be old enough and mature enough to do certain things, and there were not going to be shortcuts. They were very principled and could not be swayed by "all the other parents allow it" kind of arguments. They always stuck to their beliefs and held fast to their values.

I decided I needed to find a way to go on one of those weekend adventures that my older friends could have now that they could drive. Back then, the hub of the social universe was the

Walmart parking lot in Louisville, Mississippi, my hometown. In the way of fourteen year olds who are scared to miss out on the action, I HAD to get to the Walmart parking lot!

So I concocted what I thought was an ingenious plan. I announced early in the week that my best friend, Steven Yarbrough, and I would be camping out Friday night.

Our house was in a rural area, and you could walk across our road and go right into the woods, where we had little camp areas on our land that we sometimes used. I talked up my fake plan all week. I chattered on about how we would use all the camping skills we acquired in Boy Scouts. I said we really wanted to get in tune with nature and enjoy a night of roughing it. Yes, I laid it on thick all week.

Steven had recently gotten a Datsun 280ZX, and I thought it was the coolest car I'd ever seen. The actual plan was to hide his car down the gravel road that gave us entry to the campsite. We would depart my house, on foot, camping gear in tow, and make our way to the campsite. Once there, we would wait for sundown, and then we would be off to revel in the glories of the Walmart parking lot.

The time came for my big night, and I made an elaborate show of getting together the camping gear and heading off. All was going according to plan, and as soon as sundown came, we walked to Steven's beautiful, silver 280ZX and fired up the engine.

Everything was going perfectly—this was going to be a great night. Steven put the car in gear and we began our getaway. That is until we got to the end of the gravel road. Standing in our path was my dad.

Dad sent Steven on his way and told me to get back home. My dad could be a stern disciplinarian and often added quite a bit of volume to his lectures, but on this occasion, he didn't yell or get angry. But once back home, punishment was swift and certain. I was grounded for an entire month and lost a bunch of privileges.

At one point, I had to ask. "Dad, how did you know?"

"I knew something was up by Wednesday," he said. "No one has ever been THAT excited about one night of camping!" My dad is an extremely wise man and had a particularly good radar for when he was being fed a line of bull.

Without my fully grasping it, my mom and dad's influence and example had built a lie detector inside me. As you have already read, there were times that I did not completely live up to what they taught. But it was always there, helping me get back on the right track when I started derailing.

One of the most crucial ways it helped me was to be honest about the effort I put into anything. Great leaders learn to be totally honest about how hard they are working, and they must dial that effort up to the maximum setting.

If you are aspiring to be a business leader, here is one of the most important pieces of advice I can give you: do not count on your boss or leader to motivate or define your performance. Relying on others means you need extrinsic motivation to progress.

But only you know if you are truly giving your best effort and not cutting corners. Holding yourself accountable means your motivation is coming from inside you—it is intrinsic motivation. That is what powers great leaders.

It is also a preview of what things will look like when you do get to the top of an organization. There will be no one above you to define your performance, and all the honesty and effort will have to come out of your own drive and enthusiasm.

One example of this is what I did as a coach when it came to physical conditioning and my team. I made the decision that I was going to hold myself accountable to be in my best physical shape, even as a coach. This is what I was demanding from my players, and it would have been phony for me not to set the example.

I made it a point to jump into practices and workouts daily, ready to set the mood and pace with my effort. That might look like jumping in a 5-on-5 full-court scrimmage, actively taking part in small group instruction, or occasionally leading the team in conditioning sessions.

One example that stands out in my memory was our preseason conditioning run in 2010–2011. I wanted our team to be in outstanding shape. We had a very good team coming back and some exciting newcomers.

It was key for that team to understand how much we would rely on physical conditioning. So the tone was set by gathering one morning at 6:00 a.m. at Kentucky's football stadium, then known as Commonwealth Stadium (it's now known as Kroger Field).

This stadium seats sixty thousand people, and it has steep ramps for people to enter the stadium, and then, of course, a bunch of stadium steps. After warm-ups, we began a game of Follow the Leader.

With the sun rising, we sprinted up several steep ramps, me leading the charge. After that, we entered the stadium and sprinted up and down the stadium steps. It was a truly exhausting work out.

I am fortunate to be on an alumni group text chat with many of my former players, and one time years later I sent out a text asking about recollections about that day. Many funny comments ensued, including one from Kastine Evans. Kastine, an outstanding player from Connecticut who is now moving up the ranks of corporate America, captured the flavor of the responses when she said, "I remember Coach Mitchell acting like he wasn't sore for the next week!"

So the team certainly noticed that I wasn't as young as I used to be! But they also noticed that I pushed myself hard enough to be sore.

As their coach, I didn't possess the basketball skills these elite athletes possessed on the court. However, through an honest effort, I showed them I would be their coach and leader and never wanted them to give more effort than I was willing to give.

I could demonstrate my willingness to give effort by leading a workout, devising an excellent game plan, and teaching them the skills and importance of being a well-rounded player. In short, I couldn't play the game for them, but I could show them what honest effort looks like in a coach and leader.

As a leader of a business, you may have key players who have technical skills, marketing skills, human resource skills, or accounting skills that you don't possess. Through your leadership vision and giving an honest effort in your area of expertise, you set an example for your team that indicates the importance of honest effort.

A good question to reflect on is this: where are you asking your team or coworkers for honest effort, but are not doing it yourself? Believe me, your team will notice where you are holding them to a standard that you yourself don't meet. It is a big source of de-motivation in organizations.

CREATING A PLAN AND ENVIRONMENT WHERE EFFORT COMES FIRST

As a coach, it was my responsibility to get across to my players that much of our success was dependent on the amount of energy and effort we were willing to put in. And that meant constructing plans for practice that emphasized effort.

One way we did this is we would have times at practice where we told the players, "Right now, you are going to just play. We're not going to be worried about the rules or stopping the action. Play as hard as you can play—period."

This turned out to be a huge breakthrough for us. During these "play hard and forget everything else" times, the players went all out to the best of their ability, without overly worrying about perfection and precision. We found out that once you had 100 percent effort, you could fine-tune for precision eventually. The effort came first.

How could you do this in your business life? Perhaps you have creative meetings where everyone is encouraged to bring as many ideas to solve problems as fast as they can think of them. Nothing gets censored, nothing gets laughed at, and everything is on the table. You may produce a bunch of substandard ideas, but you will also have some great ones emerge. Encourage maximum effort, then fine-tune.

MENTAL VERSUS PHYSICAL

Here is a truth about mental versus physical effort: the mind is going to give in before the body does. This means you should work hard on strengthening your ability to be mentally tough because it is your mental side that has more power.

If you give in to the voice that says, "This is too hard, a little less effort will get the job done," you begin to lose touch with what you are truly capable of. When you don't push yourself, you'll never find your best.

The opposite is also true. When you tell yourself that you are going to stretch just a little bit farther this time, you begin to grow in power and see what you are truly capable of.

From a leadership perspective, what is interesting about this is that people are attracted to those who push themselves and inspire them to do the same. They feel your sense of purpose and honest effort, and they want in on it. Maybe not every single person, but the ones you really want on your team will gravitate to this kind of leadership.

ANXIETY ABOUT HONEST EFFORT

I have discovered—both from personal experience and from helping others—that sometimes a lack of honest effort is not about laziness.

It often has more to do with anxiety—you are not sure what to focus your efforts on. No one wants to feel like they are giving all-out effort on something that will turn out to be a waste of time. If this is happening to you, the best first step is this: figure out what you can control and what you cannot control.

Here is an example. We all know that the COVID pandemic caused supply chain headaches for many businesses and industries. When something like that happens, it is necessary to break down what you can control and what you cannot. Simply saying, "We have to work harder" in this kind of situation without any larger context is counterproductive.

Instead, first identify what you can control and what you cannot. Brainstorm alternative solutions. Look at everything. Then once you have a good understanding, you can put in honest effort where it will make the most impact.

Separating out these factors is very freeing. The higher up you climb in the world of business, the more it gets like big-time sports. Whatever your achievements were up to this point, you are expected to meet or exceed them, again and again. It creates pressure.

By separating what you can control from what you cannot, you can release a lot of anxiety and get the most out of your honest effort.

THIS IS WHAT REAL HONEST EFFORT LOOKS LIKE

For leaders, one of the most satisfying experiences is when you have someone on your team with great talent, who then combines that talent with an unreal dedication. These special team members have a burning desire to be the best, and it shows in their commitment to maximum effort.

One of my favorite examples of this kind of player is Jen O'Neill. Jen was the first McDonald's All-American to sign with Kentucky in the history of our women's basketball program. (The McDonald's All-American honor was at the time the most prestigious honor a high school player could receive.)

Jen, of course, had to be plenty talented to make that team. But it wasn't all about her talent. I guarantee you there were more physically gifted players selected. But I believe she was the most passionate, most tenacious, and most dedicated player on that All-American team.

When Jen arrived at Kentucky, I recognized quickly she had a strong desire to become the best she could be. Her unbridled passion led her to a rocky start early in her career, but she eventually settled in, matured, and became one of the best players in Kentucky history. She finished in the top ten in assists, three point shooting percentage—the list could go on for a while. She made it all the way to the top of women's professional basketball by playing in the WNBA for a time.

As I write this, Jen is playing her eighth season of professional basketball and played in the 2020 Olympic games in Tokyo for her native Puerto Rico. Her professional journey has literally taken her all around the globe.

All great accomplishments, but there's a smaller story I want to tell about Jen because it shows the character and principles behind all that success.

One day I was sitting in my office and Jen appeared with an unusual request. She was about to head into her final season at Kentucky, and she wanted to move back onto campus.

This was a strange request because none of my more experienced players wanted to do that. We always required our younger players to live on campus, where they could establish some routine and stability while they made the sometimes difficult transition from high school to college. For older players, like Jen, moving off campus was a rite of passage.

It was typically a positive progression for the players as they moved from dorm life to off-campus living which required more responsibility and helped prepare them for the "real world." Jen had lived off campus the year prior, but here she was saying she wanted to move back on campus.

I asked why.

"I want to spend every second I can working and preparing to have the greatest season our team can have, and I also want to prepare for my dream of playing professional basketball," she said.

Wow. That's the kind of thing a coach dreams of hearing. And I heard a lot more from Jen that year. What I mostly heard was the sound of the ball bouncing as I worked late in my office that was adjacent to the gym. It was Jen, putting in extra work with a teammate, or team manager, or sometimes all alone.

Not only did Jen make the sacrifice of moving back onto campus so she could better focus, but she followed through on that promise by putting in the honest effort. As a coach and leader, you want to inspire others. But sometimes you are lucky enough to have someone who inspires you.

PART TWO

WINNING TOOL #2

Hard Work

4

Hard Work

THE NUMBER OF GREAT COACHES THAT I HAVE LEARNED from in my career sometimes astounds me—I've been so fortunate. Not all of them have name recognition, but that just goes to show you that you do not have to be famous to be one of the best at what you do.

However, one person who had a big impact on me is both an amazing coach and a big name: Billy Donovan. And he deserves every bit of the name recognition he has. He will be a hall of famer at some point for sure.

As a college coach, he won back-to-back national championships at the University of Florida. As a player, he also played in the Final Four with Providence College. He is one of only four people to play in a Final Four and coach a national championship. The other three are Dean Smith, Joe B. Hall, and Bobby Knight—I would say that's pretty good company!

(Fun side note: Of that elite list, I met and learned from two of the four. During my tenure at Kentucky, I got to know and learn from the great Joe B. Hall, the coaching legend. Like I said, I have been so fortunate with mentors!)

I got to know Coach Donovan because he was head coach at Florida at the same time I was an assistant coach on the Florida women's team. As it happened, I was the only male on the women's team staff at the time, so there was no separate male locker room for just one coach. That meant I shared the locker room for the men's team, and this is where I got to meet and know Coach Donovan.

We got to be good friends. If you show him that you care about the game and that you want to get better, he is extremely generous with his time. I think that's one of the keys to his success: he spends a lot of time and energy investing in the people around him.

He would let me hang around and observe his practices, and he was even willing to spend time with me after practice to talk "X's and O's" and let me pick his brain. He was incredibly impactful on my coaching journey.

The other thing about Coach Donovan is that he loves competition. I mean *loves* it. Not just on the court either. He was always setting up contests and challenges to see if he could get any takers to compete with him. He loves to push himself to stay in great physical shape. So one day when he said he wanted to race, I said, "Sure, why not?"

He wanted us to run a mile as fast as we could and see who could do it in less time. I think our overall goal was for us to run it in six minutes or less, and this was in the Florida summer heat at noon. Let's just say that Coach Donovan did not mind making things extra challenging.

I accepted the challenge because I liked spending time with him, but I also had reason to believe I could hold my own. As a sophomore in high school, I had won the mile race at the state championship track meet. But what may have slipped my mind is that my high school triumph had been more than a decade ago, and I had gained a little weight since then. I was not as spry as I had once been.

So we headed out to the track across the street from our offices. After a quick warm up, we toed the starting line. The only thing on the line was bragging rights and the satisfaction of pushing ourselves by competing.

Billy was always in great shape, but I truly believed I could beat him in this race. The adrenaline was pumping, and I was fired up.

As soon as we took off, Billy set a blistering pace. The high school runner in me thought, *Good, he will probably wear himself out, and then I'll leave him in the dust.* I didn't realize just how in shape Billy was though. We both broke the six-minute mark on our mile run, but Billy won by a pretty healthy margin of 5–10 meters.

I probably should have been the one worrying about keeping the pace because when it was over I was suffering from heat exhaustion. Billy took no pity. He made some jokes about how it was good that the Florida Gators were sponsored by Gatorade because it looked like I would need to drink a lot of it when we got back to the office.

That's a fun memory for me (except for the heat exhaustion part), but there is more to it than just fun. There's a lesson in it too. Once you have been around enough great coaches in your life, you begin to see certain things in common. They all express it through different personalities, but the bedrock principles underneath are strikingly similar.

One thing I notice with the best coaches is that they spark the competitive fire in their players. Then they use that fire to help motivate their players to work harder than they thought they could.

Coach Donovan definitely embodied all the Winning Tools, but especially Hard Work. With his competitive challenges, his own commitment to fitness, and the intensity and caring he brought to those around him, he showed that working hard consistently is a key component to success.

COMPETITION IS A GREAT MOTIVATION TO WORK HARDER

In my own coaching career, I learned to use the spirit of competition to push myself and my coaches and my team to get better. It's one reason that we focused on making our practices so demanding at the University of Kentucky.

At practices, my coaches and I were always mindful of creating game-like conditions that would force our players to bring out the best in each other. For example, when we had a player whose skill and athleticism allowed her to dominate her teammates in practice, we would find ways to put her at a disadvantage. We might make practice six against five or even seven against five, putting the dominant player on the team with less players. This forced her to play harder and develop her skills. When you are dominating the competition fairly easily, the only thing growing is your ego.

To put it simply, real growth requires being challenged.

This is something I think is often overlooked in the business world. When most leaders think about competition, they focus on being competitive with other companies. And, of course, that is important. Ultimately, you want your team to win in your market, and you want the whole team working together to make that happen.

But to reach that end goal, there is tremendous value in thinking about how to create an environment of competition *within* your team to bring out everyone's best.

I've observed in the business world that sometimes there is a hesitancy to use competition within a company to bring out the best in everyone. There are no doubt good reasons to be cautious about the dynamics of internal competition. Of course, you never want to do something that could be perceived as favoring one person over another in an unfair way.

However, if you can introduce *healthy* competition within your team in a way that can improve everyone's skills, that can be a win for everybody. Otherwise, it is too easy to get complacent.

I suspect one of the reasons that business leaders sometimes shy from having some internal competition is because they worry about how that will impact the ability to work together as a team. This is a very valid concern.

The solution is to communicate clearly with your team that the purpose of competition is to make the whole team better in the long run. Leaders learn to be creative in setting the right balance between healthy internal competition and staying cohesive as a team.

I liked to emphasize with my players that people rarely push themselves to work as hard as they can without competition. Improvement does not happen on its own, and the more we can force ourselves into situations where we are compelled to meet challenges, the faster we will progress.

In business, this could be something as simple as splitting your sales force into two teams and having them compete. This could lead to some unexpected benefits, as some of the more experienced of your salespeople may want to help their teammates.

Mentoring and teamwork could then become an unexpected result from competition. At the end of the competition, you could bring together both teams to highlight and celebrate the overall increase in sales for the company that happened because of the internal competition.

Sales is not the only place you can use competition. For example, maybe you split people into teams to design the best marketing campaign. And you may find at the end of the competition that the winning idea can be supplemented with ideas from the campaigns that did not win. Always bring it back to how the whole team benefited from the competition.

WHY YOU CAN'T GET ANYWHERE WITHOUT HARD WORK

Obviously, I am a guy that loves sports. That includes great sports like baseball and football—I have played them, watched them, and know and respect a lot of coaches in those areas.

But basketball is my true sports love, and one of the reasons is that the game is so dynamic. Baseball and football have constant pauses built in naturally between each pitch or each snap. In basketball, the game just keeps flowing naturally from offense to defense. Short of using a precious time-out, the game is always moving, always fluid.

And that dynamic aspect of the game demands a particular kind of mindset. You are forced to be constantly adjusting. Not just from offense to defense and back again, but continuous adjustments with every pass.

As a coach, I put a lot of emphasis on defense. Players naturally enjoy offense more, and good skills on offense are what the casual fan notices more than great defense. So I had to sell players on the advantages of being a tenacious defender.

One of the ways to sell the team on defense was to explain the importance of turnover margin. (A team commits a turnover when they lose possession of the ball to the other team without ever having taken a shot.)

A study of basketball was done, and it showed that the statistic that can best predict which team will win a game is the turnover margin. To oversimplify it just a bit, if you get the other team to turn the ball over more times than you turn it over to them, there's a better chance you will win.

Our goal was to create a lot of turnovers with our tough defense, and so have the better margin. But playing great defense is extremely hard work because of the dynamic nature of basketball I mentioned above.

The key to any good defense is the positioning, where each player is on the floor in relation to the ball, the basket, and their opponents. All five players on the floor need to be in the correct position based on where the ball is. Of course, the ball is always moving.

Players needed to understand why a commitment to shifting constantly was crucial. This was because the team could be in the correct defensive position based on where the opponents were in relation to the ball. But then the ball gets passed, and everyone is immediately in the wrong position relative to the ball's new position. That requires that all five players on defense react instantly, shifting based on the new situation. Then the ball gets passed again, and another shift has to happen.

It's constant, and the only solution is to have the mental toughness and the plain old hard work necessary to do it again and again.

There is no shortcut that can reduce the need to work hard all the time on defense. Spending time at the chalkboard and watching film and talking about the principles of good defensive positioning are important. But no amount of time spent on those activities can make up for a lack of hard work in the moment. This was why I put so much emphasis on the necessity of hard work with my players on a consistent basis.

In business, you need this same sense of purpose about hard work. And this purpose and commitment to hard work needs to be communicated to all team members. Sometimes it can be easy to think that all you need is the right strategy rooted in an honest evaluation of the competitive environment you are in.

Yes, the right strategy is crucial, but if you start to think that is all you need, you will fall short. Just like in basketball, you can only stay in good position through relentless hard work. If you find yourself in too many meetings and doing too much planning, it might be time to start emphasizing the importance of pure hard work.

To develop as an excellent leader, you have to make that connection for your team. Nothing can cure the problem of being outworked. You will lose 100 percent of the time.

The first thing to ask yourself is this: what is the equivalent of defensive positioning in your business? And where can you outwork other companies in your market in a way that will make the most impact?

This is what you need to get you and your team laser focused on. Find out what the equivalent of turnover margin is for your company, and then explain to your team why you are going to outwork everyone else in the area that counts the most.

BURNOUT VERSUS HARD WORK

Great leaders learn to also know the difference between success versus obsessing about total victory.

Success is getting the best possible outcome under whatever conditions or restraints you are under. No one can control everything.

The way to burnout is to have an unhealthy obsession with defining success as always having to be number one, no matter what.

To get this point across, I like to encourage business leaders (and future leaders) to make a One Word Shift. Do not say, "I will be THE best." Instead, say, "I will be MY best." Aiming to be THE best leads to burnout and unrealistic expectations. Not everyone can be Michael Jordan. So should all the other players quit basketball because they can't be THE best?

But with the One Word Shift from "the" to "my," everything changes. You are still pushing yourself to excellence, but you are not setting yourself up with impossible goals.

This lesson came home to me during my college coaching career. There are over three hundred Division I schools in the NCAA, and every year there is only one national champion. Does that mean that only one team can have a successful season every year?

Thinking you must be the champion to be successful is a tempting way to look at it. I know because I did at times think like that. But I eventually came to realize that being the champion at the end of the year was not the only way to define success. In fact, having that as the exclusive goal could actually work against success.

It is better to focus on sustainable goals and what is right in front of you to accomplish. After I began to get some perspective over time, I would look back on seasons and see that we had many teams where everyone got the most out of themselves and the team was able to go as far as they could.

That is the way to define success. As you develop leadership skills, always keep in mind this balance between pushing people to work as hard as they can, while also recognizing when to celebrate accomplishments along the way.

5

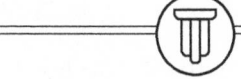

Working Efficiently

TOO OFTEN, WE CONFUSE ACTIVITY WITH ACCOMPLISHMENT.

In college basketball, the expectation was always that coaches would put in long hours, particularly during the season. This was an appropriate expectation because there was always film to watch, game plans to make, and fires to put out. Putting in a lot of hours is just part of the deal.

But I also noticed that putting in long hours could start to evolve into something else. It sometimes became less about the work and more about having a badge of honor. As if the simple act of staying at work longer than others meant that you were getting more done.

When I was a young assistant at Florida, the athletic department was one of the most decorated and celebrated in the country, ranking high in total championships across all sports (success that has been sustained over recent decades as well).

It was a tremendous culture to be in as a young, developing coach because the expectation for excellence permeated the entire department. Our leader at the time, Jeremy Foley, was a trailblazer in developing a department that emphasized competitive success among ALL sports, not just football or men's basketball. He was at that time, and remains, one of the most inspirational leaders I ever had the honor of learning from.

Because of this inspirational culture, a few of us hardworking assistants started an unspoken competition of who would be the last to leave the office at night. Looking back on it, I am so grateful for all the lessons I learned from this winning culture. But I also have to admit that I think sometimes we probably ended up wasting time at our desks in the name of "working hard."

We really did work hard, but there is a fine line that can be crossed into wanting to also show that you're working hard. In some businesses this can slip into the mentality of measuring work purely by the time you spend at work, which reveals misplaced priorities. Leaders need to cut through extraneous measures and make sure recognition and rewards are given for actually getting work done, not just for being there.

In talking with and advising business leaders, I heard a lot about how the COVID pandemic impacted all aspects of their businesses.

And one of those impacts was in many cases taking away our ability to "go to work." We found out how much we could accomplish at home or outside the office through the smart use of technology. In this environment, we could not merely spend time in our office as a sign of hard work. In this environment, it became more about what you produced than how long you "worked."

This move toward remote work may have been accelerated by the pandemic, but it was underway beforehand, and remote work is likely to continue to grow. This is going to continue to force businesses to grapple with questions of measuring productivity in more precise ways.

It also requires some self-assessment. In your own work, are you focused on how long you work or how productive you are? The difference in emphasis is crucial. In a business setting, it is productivity and the quality of the output that should be measured. The quantity of hours a person has worked, or how long they hang around the office, should not be the standard.

If you want to improve your work efficiency, start with this: ask yourself how you are measuring your own work. Is it your actual productivity and the quality of your results, or is it that your car was the last to leave the parking lot?

Getting really clear on your own expectations and how efficiently you are meeting them can bring incredible clarity to what really matters.

If you manage a team or an entire organization, you also need to be mindful of both the subtle and overt messages you are sending those who report to you. Is it clear to them that they are being judged on quality and productivity? Do they know with precision what their roles are and what they are expected to get done? Or are the standards vague, and do people think they are being judged by how much time they are spending on something?

Taking the time to think through and then set clear standards that measure efficiency, quality, and productivity is transformative for organizations. Suddenly the work is completely focused on the right things, instead of on vague feelings about who is working hard.

DOES EVERYONE KNOW WHAT ROLE THEY ARE PLAYING?

As I was working my way up through the ranks of the world of basketball coaching, I spent a lot of time as an assistant in several programs. Assistant coaches are given specific areas that they need to master, and so I developed some specialties.

For example, one of my specialties was working with post players. (For those who may not be familiar with the game, these are the players who play near the basket—centers and big forwards.) Working in this role across many jobs allowed me to become skilled in coaching this area.

Of course, I had many other roles. One of the big ones was watching hours and hours (and hours!) of game film to scout our opponents for their tendencies. Other tasks included recruiting calls, engaging with donors, and going to NCAA compliance meetings. Not all of it was fun, of course. But the times it worked best were when I knew exactly what was expected of me and what roles I was there to fulfill.

How well do you know what is expected of you in your own role at work? How could you better define it? What area could you become a super expert on that would help you advance (similar to my role as an expert working with post players)? Answering these three questions can be a game changer for your advancement at work.

If you are in a leadership position, this idea of clear roles and expectations has a whole other dimension. Instead of focusing exclusively on your own role, you need to put an emphasis on making sure everyone who reports to you knows clearly what you expect. You also need to think through how to best match the needs of a role with the right person, the one with matching skills and temperament. What will bring out each person's best work?

As a head coach, I had to learn to meet all my own expectations while making sure the rest of my coaching staff was also working efficiently and together. I found it was not something that came naturally to me. That in turn forced me to confront the number one killer of efficient work: procrastination.

BATTLING PROCRASTINATION

Here's the weird thing about procrastination. I don't think in most cases its primary cause is laziness. Sure, that may be the case for a few people. And laziness probably is at least a contributor in most cases, but I think it is a minor factor.

In my own experience, I found I was procrastinating because I have a tendency to be a *prisoner of perfectionism.*

Here's how it would play out. I'd have a project or specific area where I wanted to improve myself or my team. I would get very focused on the outcome—how it needed to be great, perfect even. To reach that fantastic result that I was imagining in my mind, I thought I needed to be in a state of inspiration to figure out how to move forward.

So I told myself I would get started when my thoughts were perfectly aligned and I knew all the exact steps to get from where my team was to that amazing result in my mind. Once I had that inspiration and was clear on everything, then I would get started.

Maybe this sounds familiar to you. I find that a lot of high achievers and ambitious people fall victim to this form of procrastination. It actually comes in part from a desire to not waste time, because we want to know exactly how we will get from point A to point B with perfect clarity and foresight. That way we won't be wasting any energy on the wrong things.

But all this is just another manifestation of that same old problem of focusing too much on the outcome we desire, instead of getting to work on the fundamentals.

If you have procrastinated yourself, you know what happened to me when I put things off. Whatever I needed to do still needed doing. But because of the delays caused by waiting for perfect inspiration to strike, the deadline snuck up on me. Now I would have to rush everything.

This, of course, creates a tremendous amount of stress. That's when mistakes happen more frequently, and the anxiety of the deadline can cause lower quality results.

In truth, many times I was able to come up with good ideas and was able to get good results, even using this unintentional "method" of procrastination, followed by the pressure of a deadline. It's just that I put myself through the ringer when I didn't need to. I would also be left wondering if I could have done even better if I didn't procrastinate.

If you are moving through the ranks in business, you may also experience what I did once you reach a high-level leadership position. After I became a head coach, I realized procrastinating becomes less and less of an option unless you want to stay stagnant, or even be demoted or lose your job. As a leader, if you procrastinate, the rest of the team is waiting on you for guidance. And then *everyone* is put under more time pressure.

This quickly becomes unworkable for any organization. You no longer have the luxury of procrastination when you become a head coach or are heading up a business team.

THE CURE

So becoming a head coach forced my hand. This problem needed to be solved, and here is what I did. First, I came up with the vision of what needed doing. It can help to write that down. But then don't spend a lot of time daydreaming about that result you want. Don't think about how it's got to be perfect. Just know where you need to go and move on to the next step.

The next step is to go backward. Work backward from the vision you have. What has to happen for the vision to come true? Get really practical here and write out the steps.

The key is then to take those steps and get organized with a plan that you map to a calendar. I prefer and recommend a paper calendar. While this is an individual preference, I do think it is truly superior to a digital calendar. It forces you to slow down a bit more and can help you think through your planning in a more deliberate way.

Whatever you use, make sure you also add in all upcoming personal dates, like family birthdays, vacations, etc. Since we aren't work robots, and we have other commitments and obligations, it's important to include these other things that will impact your time. If you fail to account for personal obligations, your plan will not be realistic.

Next, create weekly plans to accomplish your vision. What has to happen each week for your accomplishment to happen on time?

From there, take it down to the daily level and get it on your calendar. Specific weekly and daily planning will crush procrastination. Instead of some vague, daydreamed result hanging out there in the ether, you know exactly what you need to do *today*. Committing to having a daily plan with specific tasks to accomplish is life-changing. You have no chance of becoming an impactful leader unless you use your days intentionally.

THE GREATEST TIME KILLER EVER INVENTED

Has there ever been a greater destroyer of working efficiently than the internet?

Of course, I acknowledge this can cut both ways. Personal computers wired up to the internet have created so many efficiencies in our lives. But it is also one giant rabbit hole that can cost you hour upon hour if you let it.

My major weakness in this area is YouTube. I'm a big fan. I can totally justify it too! I watch things that can help me with my coaching business, including motivational videos. If I start to question myself about how much I am watching, I'll rationalize it as something that benefits the work I do.

While that may be true, the question I need to ask myself in these situations is this: "Yes, you are benefiting, but is it the *best* use of your time right now?" Because there are a lot of good things you can be doing on the internet, but that doesn't make them the best use of your time. Sometimes we have to give up something that benefits us for something that would be even better.

Just like my weakness is YouTube, maybe yours is Facebook, Instagram, Twitter, or TikTok. You tell yourself you're keeping in touch with family and friends and sharing positive things in your life. Or maybe you spend a ton of time on social media, and justify it by saying you are keeping up with the news or staying in touch with trends in your industry.

All of these things truly can be positive and don't need to be eliminated completely. Just like my use of YouTube, there are benefits. However, if you are doing these things in place of more productive things, that's when the internet becomes a procrastination-enabling machine.

The solution goes back to the daily tasks on your calendar. Those need to be the priority before videos, social media, and endlessly surfing the news. This is another reason that having a daily and weekly plan is crucial for combatting procrastination. It keeps your priorities straight.

One thing I highly recommend is blocking out time to accomplish your daily plan by completely shutting yourself off from distractions. This takes some practice and some discipline to get good at, but once you do you might be shocked by how much more you get done.

HOW YOU SPEND YOUR DAYS IS HOW YOU SPEND YOUR LIFE

When my staff and I worked with our players, we were mindful of the fact that the basketball skills we were teaching them had a limited shelf life of usefulness. It was a little bit of a unique situation for someone who teaches a skill.

English professors that teach students better reading and writing skills can be sure that they are having a lifelong impact because those skills will be incredibly useful for a person's whole life. A business teacher knows that if their students master basic business principles, that will serve them well throughout their entire careers.

But a basketball coach? Improving ball handling skills, shooting better, and getting more rebounds all add to the enjoyment and satisfaction of the game. And it is worthwhile to be truly excellent at something. However, with a few exceptions, those athletic skills will not get you hired anywhere or advance your career.

Of course, some players would go on to the WNBA, or play professionally in Europe, Asia, Australia, or South America. Some could get jobs coaching or teaching the game in some capacity. But even these generally have a time limit. No player plays forever.

As a coach, I did not want any player to be able to come back to me in ten years and say, "Coach, you taught me how to rebound better, but that has never once helped impact my career or made me better with the people around me. Why didn't you teach me something more useful?"

Of course, this is what the Winning Tools are all about in an overall sense, giving the players what they need to succeed in any area. But I wanted them to also have some very specific skills that could help them on a daily basis.

This is why we so strongly emphasized the importance of organizing and planning on a weekly and daily basis. (I will share in more detail in Chapter 7 what we did specifically.) I knew from my own experience that this habit of planning is foundational to real change. If my staff and I could help these young women implement this, it was something that they would benefit from throughout their lives.

This was not something I did when I was young—not by a long-shot. The truth is I was not much of a student, and in general I was pretty disorganized in how I approached a lot of things. I had energy and enthusiasm to burn for coaching, and that helped carry me along, but at a certain point you need to take it up a notch.

In this area, I was fortunate enough to meet Tom Nerney, who I met when he was coaching an AAU game in Las Vegas, Nevada. I was a young college assistant at the time, and I was there to scout potential recruits.

After the game, I approached Tom and proceeded to stumble through a series of poorly formulated questions about one of his players. I think Tom was slightly amused at the enthusiastic but inexperienced young man he had in front of him.

I found out Tom was a highly successful insurance executive based in Wayne, Pennsylvania, a suburb of Philadelphia. He also clearly loved the game and was an excellent basketball coach. This somewhat chance encounter led to him becoming one of the most important mentors in my life. We are still friends to this day, some twenty-plus years later.

Tom taught me so much and is one of the big reasons I was able to make the transition from assistant coach to head coach in my career. One of the most important things he taught me was planning and organization on a day-to-day basis.

This teaching had such a transformative effect in my life that now I want to share it with as many people as I can. When you get right down to the core of how we spend our lives, it is about how we spend our days. A life is the accumulation of what we are doing on a daily basis.

When you learn to control your daily plan, you will be putting yourself in control of your life.

6

Toughness

AZIA BISHOP IS ONE OF THE MOST GIFTED ATHLETES I ever had the pleasure of coaching. She came to the University of Kentucky from Toledo, Ohio, where she played high school ball. She stands an imposing 6'4". Often players this tall can be a bit slower, but Azia could also run extremely fast.

For all her skills and size, she also had a weakness. She hated taking a charge. For those not familiar with basketball, this is standing in a legal defensive position and letting the opposing offensive player run you over and knock you backward onto the hardwood court. The offense gets called for a foul, but you get run over. Sounds fun, right?

Well, fun or not, it was a major part of our overall defensive strategy and game planning at Kentucky. Azia's dislike of taking a charge would not have been a problem at a lot of college basketball programs. Not many teams make taking a charge an emphasis, so this set us apart and helped make our reputation for having a tough and tenacious defensive style.

Azia certainly was not the only one of our players not thrilled about it. Players know that you get on the highlight reel by dunking, nailing three-point shots, and great no-look passes. Let's just say taking a charge does not usually make the top ten plays of the day on SportsCenter. Teaching players to love taking a charge was often a hard sell.

But even if Azia was not alone in disliking it, she stood out for how much she hated it.

She reasoned that as tall as she was, she could be blocking shots instead of standing in the way and letting someone run her down. "Why can't I just swat these balls away?"

I could understand why it looked that way from her point of view. But we had done the statistical analysis, and it showed us that getting into a legal position to take a charge gave us better results. When we took a charge, the ball would immediately be blown dead, and we would now be on offense. Everything about this defensive scheme fit well with our overall model of being a team that was fast and athletic. So we discouraged shot blocking and practiced taking charges.

We taught the proper technique again and again in practice. When you use the correct method to take a charge, you will not get injured. But that's not the same thing as saying it won't hurt. Because getting knocked backward onto the floor does not feel great. Azia suffered through the drills, and my coaching staff and I did our best to continue emphasizing its importance.

But then Azia would get into a game, and when an opportunity for a charge happened, she would instead step back and try to block the shot. This often led to her fouling, and she would have to come to the bench in foul trouble. So then she adjusted and would make a half-hearted attempt at taking a charge, and this just earned her more fouls. If you do not commit fully to taking the charge, the foul is going to be called on you.

This pattern went on for a while, and Azia really struggled with it. Then one day at practice Azia told me, "Coach, I am going to take a charge in our next game." This surprised me because, to say the least, the next game on our schedule would be a tough one to take your first charge.

We were going to be playing the University of Tennessee. Sadly, Pat Summit had retired due to an illness that would eventually take her life. But the tradition she had built proudly carried on, and Tennessee was still the gold standard in women's college basketball. On top of that, this game was going to be on the road in Knoxville. The University of Tennessee *almost never* lost at home; it is an incredibly tough place to play in front of their devoted fans. And on top of all that, those Tennessee teams were just super hard-nosed and aggressive. That was the style Pat Summit taught, and those were the kind of players she recruited. That had not changed.

If you were going to pick a place and a team to finally get the courage to take a charge, this was one of the most challenging circumstances to do it. I was thrilled to hear her willingness, and I encouraged her, saying, "I really believe if you do that, Azia, we are going to win this game."

Game time came, and we were playing excellent basketball. We were close to being able to pull off the road upset, and at a crucial point in the game a Tennessee player drove hard toward the basket.

And, lo and behold, there is Azia Bishop in perfect position to take the charge. And she does not flinch. The Tennessee player runs her over aggressively. The whistle blows.

Azia has just taken the first charge of her college career.

What made the play particularly beautiful was her textbook positioning to take the charge. The referee really could not have called it any other way. It was just that well done.

It was an amazing coaching moment, watching her make that sacrifice and meet the challenge. But what happened next was even better. In fact, it was one of the most satisfying moments in my entire coaching career.

Our bench just absolutely exploded with excitement and cheering for Azia. These women, her fellow teammates, had been with her to all those practices. Every one of them knew it was a difficult obstacle for her to surmount. They knew full well what a challenge it was for her to rise up to that moment and show the toughness necessary to get run over. It helped us win that game, in the place where almost no road team ever wins.

I remember how sweet the feeling was to later watch the game highlights from the TV broadcast. The TV crew noticed and captured how our bench went insane with joy for their teammate making a defensive play. It just brought everything together for me. Teammates taking great pride and happiness in the success of another. A team that had fully bought into our unusual defensive scheme. And a young woman keeping her promise to me to take a charge in the game and growing in the process.

It is said that your life flashes before your eyes as you leave this world for the next. If that happens to me, I am sure that this will be included in my highlight reel. Just an amazing, unforgettable moment for a coach.

There are several lessons that can be drawn out of that story, but there is one I want to highlight for the purposes of this chapter: people are not born tough; they develop toughness by making choices.

It may be true that some people find making that choice for toughness easier than others. We all have different personalities, life experiences, and overall circumstances that can make choosing toughness easier or harder.

But that does not change the fact that you can choose to develop toughness. Too many people think it is either something you are born with or you weren't. But as the example of Azia demonstrated, you can choose to become tougher.

Now let's get a little more specific and talk about five qualities that reveal a person who chooses toughness:

#1 Hears Constructive Criticism

No one likes bad news about themselves, but a person who is tough chooses to hear criticism and objectively analyzes it. If you are the kind of person who gets defensive easily, you need to start making a conscious choice to *invite* criticism. Proactively ask people for feedback on what you could be doing better.

Practice listening for the facts behind the critique and dealing with those facts without emotion. When you get into a leadership position, this kind of toughness becomes even more important. People will shy away from direct, honest feedback to "the boss" for fear of reprisals. Exemplifying the tough-mindedness to hear constructive criticism will go a long way toward building a culture of success.

#2 Pushes through the Boring Parts

Every job has duties that are boring or painful or both. You will probably not be surprised to hear that some of the tasks around recruiting and NCAA compliance were dull. Watching lots and lots of game film has some good moments of insight, but I found myself having to push through long hours of it.

No matter what job you have, what business you run, or what goal you have, you know exactly what I mean. Your tedious tasks are different ones, no doubt, but the idea is the same. No career worth having and no goal worth pursuing can be accomplished without a certain amount of work that is tedious and hard to force yourself to do.

However, the more you can train yourself to plunge ahead and get it done with quality and timeliness, the better your results and the more respect you will earn from others. Think of this element of toughness as similar to a choice to stick to a workout schedule, especially on days you do not feel like it.

When you make the choice to work out when you do not feel like it, you are building a certain kind of habit that makes that choice a little more likely next time. When you choose not to, you make it easier to skip again the next time.

#3 Avoids Cruise Control

One of the themes throughout this book has been focusing on qualities of character—honesty, hard work, discipline—instead of obsessing about results. One of the main reasons for that is our natural tendency for wanting to put things on cruise control, especially when things are going okay.

Maybe you are right on target for meeting your quarterly sales quota, or maybe even a little ahead. The inclination is to ease back a little. No sense busting your butt if you do not have to.

A lot of times you do not notice this easing up or you rationalize it. It is a form of toughness that only the best leaders have, to push themselves and others even when already at the top. Because that is how you stay on top.

#4 Does Not Get Caught Up in Preseason Polls

Preseason polls used to drive me crazy when I was a coach. I understand why they are done; fans love their sports and love to think about and debate the upcoming season. The media responds to this interest with things like preseason polls and predictions.

There are some 330 or so Division I women's basketball teams, and these polls create the Top 25 of them before a single shot has been launched toward the basket. There are also the conference previews that supposedly tell you where a team is likely to finish in those standings. I am not saying these polls are always way off, but they can be wildly wrong for a lot of teams.

As a coach, these polls are not your friend. If your team is predicted to be awesome, you have to spend a lot of time constantly reminding the players that the prediction is meaningless in terms of earning wins. You still have to go out on the court and prove it with your actions because that poll is as worthless as the paper it was printed on (or I guess now, as worthless as the digital pixels on a screen).

Predictions for a low finish also are not very helpful. You could use it as "we'll show them" motivation, but in general, I think when people hear outside voices telling them they have low expectations, it can be easier than you think to start believing them.

What does this have to do with toughness? It is about training your mindset to ignore outside voices—whether they are applauding you or being negative, and instead keeping laser focused on what you need to do. Of course, I am not talking here about valid feedback, but about distracting voices that do not have any basis for making a solid judgment.

Your business no doubt has its own version of preseason polls. These are the expectations, the sales forecasts, the payroll numbers that you have to hit. I am sure in many cases they are grounded in good data and sound predictions.

I am also sure that any number of things can happen during the course of the fiscal year to blow these predictions up. And I am even more sure if you just assume that you will beat last year's numbers because you have done that the past three years, you are courting trouble.

Predictions will not be doing the work for you. Tough-minded leaders do not let predictions get into their head, and they purposely guide their teams to focus on the fundamentals in front of them instead of pointless distractions.

#5 Exhibits Resilience

Who do you think of when you hear the word "resilience"?

Of course, I do not know who you will say, but I do know this: I am sure you admire them. Resilience is that form of toughness that lets us endure hardships, reversals, unexpected challenges, and embarrassing moments and yet still keep showing up and doing our best. It is a universally admired quality.

You will become more resilient by watching others who have endured misfortune or a poor life choice and found ways to overcome it, or at least not be defeated by it. The more you observe someone else who has chosen resilience, the more you will know that you are capable of it.

Look for mentors in your life who are older and have been through more. They have seen the business downturns when the future looked bleak and then survived to thrive later. They have made mistakes that they had to acknowledge, fix, and then get on with the next task.

They *chose* toughness and resilience, and they can share their wisdom with you.

This chapter started with a story about one of my players learning about toughness. Let's end it on another story about a player that reminded me what resilience looks like and how inspiring it can be when you have a front row seat to watch it.

Bria Goss was a physically tough player at Kentucky. But she stood out because that toughness also extended to her mental and emotional sides. She truly had one of the most amazing attitudes I have witnessed, and she never seemed to get down.

It was a joy to coach her, and it was great to have her steady presence on the team. However, my clearest memory of Bria, the one that sums her up to me, is about a time she screwed up badly. Or, to be more precise, I remember how she responded to messing up.

It was the end of a close game, and the arena was packed with eight thousand–plus people. She was fighting to secure a ball that was loose, and when she got a hold of it, she signaled for a time-out to make sure we kept possession. That's usually a smart play.

There was only one problem. We did not have any time-outs left. By rule, that is a technical foul. The other team gets to shoot two free throws and then is also awarded the ball. (Many of you probably have seen the famous play when Chris Webber from the University of Michigan made this same mistake at the end of a national championship game.)

This is an extremely bad mental error for a player to make, and it can be especially costly at the end of a close game. It is hard on a player to make a mistake like this, especially in a team sport. You can feel like you let your teammates down, and then there are thousands and thousands of witnesses to your mistake in the stands. Imagine making a huge blunder at your work and having that many people instantly see it.

What has always stuck with me about the moment is that Bria did not hide from it, but she also did not make a big, dramatic scene either. She took responsibility verbally by acknowledging it was a mistake, and then she turned her focus back to helping us win the game. I'm not sure many people twice her age would have handled it with that much resilience, but here was a young person showing what a truly tough attitude looks like.

Guess who ended up making the final defensive play of the game that sealed the win for us? Yes, Bria Goss.

These are the benefits of developing toughness. In a moment of a big, public mistake, Bria had the inner resources to keep steady to the team's purpose, and then she did not flinch when we needed her at the end.

A good question to ask yourself is whether you would be able to do the same with a mistake at work. Could you acknowledge it, take responsibility for it, and then have the resilience to get mentally and emotionally right back to your purpose?

There is a temptation when others know you messed up to make it all about you. Yes, you take responsibility, but then you want to show everyone how upset you are about it. Or you acknowledge it, but then keep throwing in excuses and subtle reasons why you really should not be blamed.

You and your team will be better off if you handle it with tough-minded resilience. In other words, handle it like Bria would.

PART THREE

WINNING TOOL #3

Discipline

7

Discipline

WHENEVER I TELL PEOPLE I WORKED FOR PAT SUMMIT as a graduate assistant at the University of Tennessee, it almost always grabs people's attention. She was such a legendary coach and personality, everyone wants to know what she was like and what I learned from her.

There is something about the elite-of-the-elite coaches that fascinates us. I think if I had told people I had worked for John Wooden, or Vince Lombardi, or Joe Torre, or any other amazing coach, they would wonder the same thing.

Two things come immediately to mind about Coach Summit. One is more of a fun story, and the other is about a particular quality I noticed that I think was one of the big reasons for her greatness. But both in their way show her ability to channel her presence and intensity to get results.

The fun story happened just after I was hired to become an assistant at the University of Tennessee. I was a graduate student assistant, so I was on the lowest rung of the ladder. The first experience I had with the team was being along for a summer tour with them in Europe. We were there for ten days and played five games.

Then we got back to Knoxville at the end of August, and this was my first day at the office. I had my little cubicle, and I figured it would be a happy year for me even if they kept me in the corner, and I spent the year listening and learning. I did not expect to have a ton of interaction with Coach Summit or think she would engage with me very much. Like I said, I was at the bottom of the office ladder.

So who do I see striding toward my cubicle on that very first day? Coach Summit. "Matthew, I need you to drive me to Bristol [a city in Tennessee]. A plane was supposed to fly me to an event, but there's something wrong with it."

She explained she was already behind and would have to do work as I drove her. I jumped up and off we went. We climbed into her amazing Mercedes. The thing felt like it was about twenty feet long—it was so huge it made me think of a yacht. A dealership had given it to her after one of her many national championships.

It was supposed to be a two- or three-hour drive, but true to her personality, she wanted to be there in half the time. And the whole time I am driving, I can remember her doing three things. One, she had a stack of things that needed autographing, and she was signing away. Two, she was on the phone a lot.

Now this was back in the early days of cell phones, and not many people had them. But she did, and that thing was always ringing. People wanted to hear from Coach Summit. Everybody wanted to pick her brain; she was just so respected. I swear I do not think I would have been shocked had the president of the United States called her while she was sitting next to me. I do not remember who all she talked to that day, but she was just always in motion.

The third thing I remember her doing was saying, "Matthew, you have to go faster." Coach had quite a reputation for fast driving, and I can confirm that is more than just a legend. So I pushed the gas pedal harder, and we climbed up past seventy and then on up to eighty. "Matthew, I really need to get to this event, and we are already late. You have to speed it up."

Up to ninety we climbed. Finally, she just said, "Matthew, you have to put the pedal to the metal." Just as I start to hit triple digits, the blue lights of the Tennessee Highway Patrol are in my rearview mirror. I pull over.

"Don't say anything, Matthew, I'll handle everything," Coach Summit told me.

I roll down the window as the trooper gets out of his car and puts on his hat and approaches the car. He is surprised to see Coach Summit. "Coach, what are y'all doing out here in August? I know you ain't playing basketball today."

She explains that she is needed in Bristol for a big booster event.

He says, "Well, y'all are going a little fast, though, aren't you?"

"I know. This boy [pointing at me] is scared to death," she says. "This is his first day on the job. This is all my fault. I really need to be there, and I kept telling him to go faster."

"If you really need to get there, it sounds like I should give you an escort into town," the trooper says. "You don't happen to have a basketball with you, do you? One you could sign?"

Coach Summit got right out of the car, and she had something like ten basketballs in the trunk. She signed it and handed it to the trooper, and we got an escort into Bristol, Tennessee.

As we followed our escort, I said to Coach, "That was lucky you had some basketballs with you."

She looked at me like I was a bit slow on the uptake. Then she said, "Matthew, that wasn't luck, that was preparation. Always be prepared."

That's a funny story that gives you a little flavor of Pat Summit. But there is something more serious I would like to share. Whenever someone asks me about what I learned from Coach Summit, I could go on forever. But one thing really stands out for me.

It was her total presence, focus, and attention to detail at practices.

Being that she was a human being, like the rest of us, you can be absolutely sure that she had outside stresses like all of us do. Everyday worries about remembering that she needed to call this person or visit that person, or all of her upcoming media obligations, or recruiting, or the book she was writing.

She was at the height of her fame and importance in American culture. Everyone wanted to talk to her, and she was constantly managing an incredibly full schedule.

Yet still, somehow, for the two to three hours of practice every day, she was completely *there*. No matter what ups and downs may have been happening outside the lines of the court, her focus was *in the moment* during practice. It was all about what can we do *today* to be successful. She was totally devoted to being present in practice for her players each and every day.

It is something I promised myself that I would try to emulate if I ever got in a high-level position to lead people. I did eventually get that chance. I could not "out-Summit" Coach Summit on this—I am not sure anyone could. But even just shooting for that high standard taught me a lot and gave me something to always reach for.

What this showed was the tremendous discipline of Coach Summit, which brings us to the third Winning Tool. I like to refer to Discipline as "the glue." Without it, everything falls apart.

The first two Winning Tools only become truly powerful when practiced consistently. Most people can be honest some of the time, maybe even a majority of the time. And most people can find it in themselves to work hard for stretches at a time, particularly when under some kind of deadline or pressure.

But that is not enough. Being honest sometimes and working hard occasionally are not going to get you the results you want. These first two tools only become super powerful when we use them consistently. And to do that, the third Winning Tool is necessary. Discipline is the tool that activates the other two. It's the glue that holds all the tools together.

When you can train yourself to be honest and work hard consistently, then you will start seeing absolutely amazing results.

This is one of the biggest lessons I learned in my own life. I went from a young person who was adrift to a successful Division I basketball coach. It certainly did not happen overnight, and even today I do not claim perfection by any stretch. But I definitely learned over the years that discipline is the key difference between ordinary achievement and getting to the top of your field.

It might help to make my point clearer to take you back to that somewhat confused young man I was decades ago. I had graduated from college and was trying to find my way in the world without really having found something I wanted to do. I was knocking around in the construction trade, trying to get into building and contracting. It wasn't really going anywhere, in part because you had to have a head for numbers, which was never my strong suit.

One night I was back at my old high school to attend a football game. Just a few years before, I had been out on that same field as a player. Maybe I had gravitated back there in part because my purpose had seemed clearer back then. Whatever the case, I found myself after the game helping my former basketball coach and the principal of my high school, Coach Farrel Rigby, clean up the stands after the game. It was just the two of us, and we got to talking.

You never know what is going to change your life. Sometimes it happens when you are picking up sticky soda cups late on a Friday night and stuffing them into trash bags. As we were discussing what I was doing at that point in my life, Coach Rigby said, "Have you ever thought about coaching? I always thought you would be good at it."

Actually, I had thought about coaching when I was in high school. When I was a teenager, my parents gave me Rick Pitino's book called *Born to Coach*, and I found it extremely inspiring. I loved sports, so coaching seemed like a natural fit for me.

But whenever I mentioned it to people, they always said you can't make a good living at coaching. So I decided I would build a construction empire instead. That was not going well, however. It did not match my life purpose, and I was miserable.

So I was in the right frame of mind to hear Coach Rigby's suggestion about coaching. It lit a fire inside, and we started discussing the possibilities. The next day we talked more and by the end of that conversation, I was the new assistant boys' basketball coach at my old high school for the 1995–1996 basketball season.

The following year I got the head basketball coaching job at Central Holmes Christian School in Lexington, Mississippi. During the summers I found myself at Pat Summit's camp, and things continued to develop along each step of the way. In fact, they developed to the point that I ended up buying the house near the University of Kentucky that used to belong to the same Coach Pitino whose book originally inspired me!

I have always felt that it was a neat circle that I ended up in the house of the person whose book I read all those years ago. (And, by the way, no matter how long I live there, locals will always refer to it as Coach Pitino's house!)

That quick summary of my coaching journey sounds kind of smooth in retrospect, but in reality the young man that I was had a long way to go to become a good leader. I found what I wanted to do, but I did not have the necessary discipline yet.

That would grow and develop over the years. In truth, it is not something you ever completely master, so I work on making discipline a choice every day.

This chapter and the following two are the important things I have learned about being disciplined since I began that journey at a high school football stadium twenty-five-plus years ago.

TEACHING PLAYERS DISCIPLINE

As you might imagine, coaching young people away from home for the first time involves a lot more than what happens on the court. These kids come to the program as teenagers, fresh out of high school. At eighteen and nineteen they are technically adults, but we all know they are still forming who they are going to be. I know I sure was at that age.

Besides adjusting to life away from home and being in a new social environment with new kinds of peer pressure, student-athletes have the higher academic demands of college and the rigorous practice and game schedules of big-time college sports.

They had to balance all these demands, which made teaching these students the power of discipline essential. And we needed to do it right from the beginning of their college life so they did not fall behind. One of the most important things we would do is have weekly Sunday night meetings with the players early in the semester.

All the coaches were there, along with the team's director of operations and an academic counselor. So besides having a lot of support on hand, it also ensured that the players had a structured and dedicated time to look at the week ahead. This is how discipline begins—by setting aside time to set yourself up for success.

At these meetings, we would get into the nitty gritty details with the players. I would give the practice schedule for the week. We would have them add it to their class schedule. We would help them plan out study time and other obligations. We encouraged them to do this on a paper calendar. This creates a slower, more deliberate method than entering it into a digital calendar. We intentionally did not want them to be in a hurry doing this, so they could see how important planning is, and that doing it more deliberately has a benefit.

The other thing we would do is later follow up to connect their accomplishments and positive experiences with the fact that they had taken the time to plan their week.

Not only would we make sure we praised them for a good grade, a compliment they received from someone on campus, or an act of kindness—we would take it a step further and tie it back to being calm and collected at the beginning of each week.

Being settled on what you have to do for the upcoming week gives such a feeling of freedom and control over your week. If you start implementing this, you are going to want to keep doing it.

This exact same strategy can turbocharge your success in business. Start by setting aside dedicated and structured time each week to think through what you need to accomplish. You should be deliberate about it and not rush through it. You should then check in with yourself daily and make sure you know what you need to accomplish each day.

You also need to find ways to praise and reward yourself for executing well, and be accountable to yourself when you fall short. If you are already in a leadership position, you need to encourage those you manage to do the same. Consider adding an "all-hands" Monday morning staff meeting to talk through what specifically needs to be accomplished that week.

Of course, you will make allowances for who you are supervising and what you should reasonably expect from them. In terms of expectations for discipline, you're not going to coach a mid-level manager with decades of experience the same way you would a summer intern.

Age, experience, and job performance expectations will impact how you coach someone to be more disciplined. But whatever modifications you make to adjust to your unique situation, the principles behind instilling this discipline don't change. That's the crucial point. Here are those principles:

- Have dedicated and structured time set aside to go through your plan for the upcoming week (and also for your day).

- Use a calendar to lock in your planning.

- Create ways to give feedback on how well the plan is being executed. You need to do this for your own plan, and if you are managing others, also find the best ways to monitor and give feedback on execution to your team.

If you institute these principles repeatedly, you will become a disciplined person and the benefits will be enormous.

LOVING WHAT YOU DO AND THOSE YOU SERVE IS AWESOME, BUT...

Wow, I love the University of Kentucky. My family and I have stayed in the area even after my retirement. I loved my players, my coaches, and the community. My bond with the university is a real emotional thing for me, and I always put my whole self into it.

On one level, this is great and totally appropriate. If you do not love what you do and who you are serving, you need to think through making a serious change. You need to love something to get out of bed in the morning and give it your best.

I also naturally like to connect with people and form bonds with them. That is also a good thing, and it has served me well.

But on another level, I needed to separate those emotions from what I needed to do to be the most effective coach I could be. I had to discipline myself to not let emotions overwhelm good decision-making.

I had to make sure that my love for all of these things did not override my ability to properly evaluate players and the state of the program. This immediately brings to mind a great leader I learned from at Kentucky, Jason Cummins.

Jason served a twenty-year career with the US Army as an Apache helicopter pilot, with tours in Iraq and Afghanistan. After his military service, he worked in the area of leadership development, and we were fortunate to have him consult with our team for several seasons.

One of the tools he introduced to our program was something he learned in the Army as a pilot. They would conduct "after action reviews" once a mission was completed. This kind of review had a very purposeful design that could be used to assess the three phases of any action. You would evaluate each phase—preparation, execution, and result—during an after action review.

What made this an extremely useful tool was that it created a special set-aside time to assess things without emotion or attachment. Forget how you feel about something and just ask what actually happened. Analyze the good, the bad, and the ugly.

This is exactly the spirit you want to have when evaluating your people and processes. Without a doubt, Jason loves the United States and proudly served his country. But when it came time to honestly assess an operation, he would not let the love and emotion overwhelm good judgment.

I hope you love what you do and care for the people who work for and with you. Just have the discipline to not let it impact your business and performance analysis.

DISCIPLINE YOURSELF TO BE CONFIDENT ABOUT WHO YOU ARE

As I said earlier, the number of amazing coaches I have learned from truly fills me with gratitude and amazement at my good fortune. And not all of them were basketball coaches.

Rich Brooks was the head coach of Kentucky's football team from 2003 to 2009. When he first got there, the program was at a low point, on probation and with only forty-nine scholarship players. He turned the program around with incredible speed. Our time at Kentucky overlapped a couple of years, and we got a chance to spend some time together. He must have made me laugh a couple of thousand times—just a great guy to be around.

But it was more than his great sense of humor that I loved about Coach Brooks. You always know where you stand with him because he has an exceptionally direct style of communication. You don't have to guess what he is thinking, and you'll never get a line of bull from Rich Brooks.

I discovered this soon after we met. His direct approach taught me a lesson that I have never forgotten and that helped me become a better leader.

Here's how I came to learn that lesson.

The University of Kentucky is, of course, a huge deal in the state. A lot of state universities have great fan bases, but Kentucky is without doubt one of the best and most intense.

So there was always demand among our supporters, boosters, and fans to see us, and so my very first year, before I'd ever coached a game at Kentucky, we barnstormed the state in what was called the Big Blue Caravan. We got on a bus and traveled to all corners of the state. As part of the caravan we participated in golf scramble tournaments with boosters.

After the golf, there would inevitably be a dinner or cookout with these supporters, and it was expected that the coaches would say a few words. I had just been hired, and my speech was along the lines of, "I'm lucky to be here and so grateful for the opportunity." And then I would emphasize again that "I'm just fortunate to be here."

Rich Brooks was along on this trip, and he had now heard me deliver these same remarks two times on successive nights. Before the next night, he finally took me aside, and with that very direct style of delivery, he told me the straight truth.

"Look, you have to stop all this stuff about 'I'm just fortunate to be here.' And I'll tell you why. Because sooner or later people are going to take you at your word and believe you just got lucky. You're the head coach at the University of Kentucky, and you need to act like this is where you belong. Stop all the other stuff." (Coach Brooks's version might have had a few extra colorful words in it, but this is an accurate summary!)

As soon as he said it, I knew he was exactly right. Basically he was giving me a great lesson in humility and disciplining yourself to see and talk about yourself accurately. True humility is not about thinking less of yourself or always saying, "Aw shucks, I don't know how little ole me got here." No, because in a way, that is just as inaccurate as bragging or thinking you know it all.

One of the keys to discipline is learning to have an accurate view of yourself and others and to express it properly. Coach Brooks also reminded me of my father in that moment. My dad was always straight ahead about what he said, without trying to shade things based on what he thought might sound right or what people wanted to hear.

Coach Brooks reminded me that I did not need to feel shy about being confident in my vision for the basketball program and to have the discipline to present myself that way consistently.

8

Attitude
is a Choice

HERE IS A CHALLENGE FOR ANY COLLEGE BASKETBALL coach: convince young, still-maturing players to put in maximum effort during summer conditioning sessions.

These are college-age women; there are other things they would rather be doing. And the season is still months away, so they wonder how important this could be. Of course, as a coach, I knew that the edge we got in conditioning in the summer would pay dividends during the season. It also starts building the habit of hard work. But all this was a tougher sell to the players because the payoff was not going to be immediate.

When you have this kind of dilemma, what often happens is you have a couple of players who start to become vocal in questioning the necessity of what they are doing. This then typically morphs into outright complaining, things get contagious, and pretty soon everyone has a sour attitude.

You have to proactively stop this kind of situation before it has a chance to get started. The way my staff and I did it was to emphasize that attitude was a choice, and a University of Kentucky women's basketball player was encouraged to choose a positive attitude.

This is an absolutely fundamental part of being a disciplined person: understanding that attitude is a choice, and then making the consistent choice to have a positive attitude toward your work, others, and your life. If you can master choosing to bring a good attitude to everything you do, it will be life-changing. I guarantee it.

FIRST THINGS FIRST

Before we get into some of the more practical aspects of this, we need to lay a foundation. Until you truly believe that attitude really *is* a choice, you cannot make progress.

Back in Chapter 5, I introduced you to one of my most important business and life mentors, the insurance executive Tom Nerney. Attitude was another area of life where I learned an enormous amount from Tom. We spent a ton of time talking about attitude. It became clear that he—who has earned so much success himself—considered it absolutely critical to high achievement.

He also introduced me to a quote by Charles Swindoll that has been on every one of my office walls since: "Life is 10 percent what happens to you and 90 percent how you react to it."

What I like about this quote is that it does not claim that we control 90 percent of our life. It says the key is how we *react* to what happens around us—in other words, *our attitude.* When you think about it, our reaction to a situation is really the only thing we can always choose to control. Once you grasp this and start making the choice for a good attitude, you will see how it gives you a feeling of tremendous freedom.

Once you are convinced that a consistently good attitude is a worthy goal, you might start wondering, "How do I do that when things go wrong or get really hard?"

Great question. Here are five answers:

#1 Repair Your Roof When It Is Sunny

One of the most impactful quotes I ever encountered has been attributed to the great Abraham Lincoln, the sixteenth president of the United States. He said, "The best time to repair the roof is when the sun is shining." This wise saying is applicable to so many areas of life, but I think is especially useful in thinking about building up your "good attitude muscle."

Being human, it is natural for our attitude to be better when the sun is shining. When things are generally going our way or are not too difficult, it is easy to kind of float along and not think about attitude too much one way or the other.

During these times, we tend not to be intentional about having a great attitude. What most of us do is still complain here and there when a little thing doesn't go our way. We don't really have a bad attitude, because overall things are going well, but we are also still in the habit of whining or letting small things get to us.

Then a big storm hits. Some heavy adversity gets between us and our goal, or a piece of bad luck or news sends us into a spiral. Suddenly, our attitude goes from decent to terrible.

This is when we tell ourselves, "Well, who wouldn't have a bad attitude under these circumstances?" I will tell you who. People who worked on maximizing having a good attitude when the sun was still shining. They worked on not complaining about the small stuff during the good times, realizing it would prepare them to have a positive attitude when the heavy weather hit.

They built up that "good attitude muscle" in every little interaction and through every small adversity. It gives them the foundation to continue to bring an amazing attitude even when truly tough times strike. Speaking of which, adversity always does strike.

#2 Expect Adversity

Why do we always underestimate how hard it is going to be to accomplish something worthwhile? Why do we map out a smooth journey in our heads to any goal we have? We are all capable of having this naïve optimism that we can go step-by-step to a huge accomplishment, with everything going as expected.

Back when I was coaching, I used to draw a mountain on the dry erase board for my team when explaining where we wanted to go. I was probably the world's worst dry erase board artist, but that never stopped me from making my point.

I'd talk about us being at the bottom of the mountain. From there we looked up and saw a big climb, but the path of ascent looked clear and smooth. But then we started moving up the mountain, and we ran into a huge boulder in the middle of the path, something that we could not see when we were standing at the base of the mountain. We would have to find a way around it.

"We do not know what is going to pop up to block us from climbing to the top, but we know something will," I told them. "When it does, we are going to have the discipline to keep good attitudes, because we are preparing every day to make that choice."

You know in your career that similar things happen. It is never the smooth ascent we see at the bottom of the mountain. That's why there are expressions like Murphy's Law—"Whatever can go wrong, will go wrong." So underneath our naïve optimism, we do know the unexpected will happen.

But despite knowing this, we still sigh, and then bemoan the problems that spring up. Work on becoming the kind of person who does not waste time fretting over obstacles.

Be the person who says, "Yes, I did not know exactly what the next obstacle was going to be, but I knew one was coming. I cannot wait to use this challenge to grow." It will transform you into a leader that people want to follow.

#3 Challenges Get Harder the Higher Up the Mountain You Climb

One of the things that made my job as a college coach interesting was helping our young players make the transition from high school to college. Any player that is recruited to an SEC school, especially a school like the University of Kentucky, was the star of their high school. Most of the time they had been the best player on the court in any game they played.

These players were so specially gifted athletically that they could overwhelm people with their physical talent. They were the center of attention, and often success came relatively easy on the court.

Now they walk into a situation at college where for the first time in their lives, they are competing against others who have a very similar physical skill level. They come to the realization very quickly that overwhelming an opponent with sheer physical talent is no longer an option. Now they had to adjust, and that meant most of them needed help learning to bring a consistently good attitude to conditioning, to practice, and to mental preparation.

Sometimes in the beginning and middle of this journey it was tough. My staff and I would spend so much time preaching these concepts, especially the necessity to discipline yourself to bring a good attitude every single day. And it often took longer for a player to take this insight to heart than I would have liked.

This forced me as a leader to discipline myself to have realistic expectations. I knew from my own journey that developing a consistently good attitude is hard work; it takes time and maturity. We are talking about eighteen- to twenty-two-year-old people who are still figuring out who they are and with the additional pressures of adjusting to a new environment. Why should I have expected an instant transformation?

In the bigger picture, one of the most satisfying parts of my coaching days was seeing the transformation when a young woman who had come in as an undisciplined freshman left as a senior who knew that attitude was a choice and that she could make the right decision on a consistent basis.

It made the times all worth it when they would sometimes look at me like I was from Mars when I was trying to instill these concepts. They thought their coaches were there to teach them to dribble, shoot, rebound, and play defense better. They're thinking, "What's all this other stuff about honesty, hard work, and discipline all the time?"

We were there, of course, to teach them to improve their basketball skills, but more importantly to give them these life fundamentals—the Winning Tools—that would make them better players but also prepared for life.

As I mentioned in Chapter 3, I'm on an alumni group chat with about twenty of my former players. We use it for things like wishing each other a happy birthday and making each other laugh and things like that. But sometimes one of them will mention something they carried over into their life and careers that came directly from the Winning Tools.

I'll hear things like, "We didn't understand why you were always on us about making a weekly plan and staying organized, but now that I use that to be successful in my job, I appreciate it." Or "I didn't know why you insisted that we were always early to class, but now people at my work notice that I am early and prepared for meetings."

It is when you hear things like this that you realize the true satisfaction of coaching and leadership is not about wins or extra profits; it is about the impact you can have on people's lives (including your own!).

#4 Accept That You Will Sometimes Fail

As the above makes clear, disciplining yourself to have a good attitude no matter the outward circumstances is hard. That means unless you are superhuman, you are going to fall short sometimes.

In fact, as you are building this "good attitude muscle" initially, you will fail more frequently. When you understand this, it is easier to accept and easier to avoid letting yourself spiral into regret and self-accusation.

Instead of beating yourself up endlessly, you just simply hold yourself to account (back to the Honesty Tool). Tell yourself you let your emotions in the moment dictate your reaction and attitude instead of controlling your own reaction through intention. Then tell yourself to turn your attitude around and do better the next time.

#5 The Proof is in How You Feel and the Results You Get

Shortcomings and temporary failures aside, I can 100 percent promise you that working on a consistently good attitude will pay extraordinary dividends across your life.

Your ability to achieve and attain goals will greatly improve, and that is rewarding. But the most convincing proof for why you should discipline your control of your attitude is not for the success or honors it will bring.

It's the feeling you get inside, a feeling that you are a more powerful, stronger, and happier person. Because you are. You now have the power over how you react to circumstances, so nothing can get you down for long.

Your happiness increases because the person you live with every second of your life (you) knows how to bring a positive attitude. And you are also happier because you are the kind of person who attracts others of a similar mindset. You end up giving what you get.

Once you start seeing these inner results, you are not going to want to stop. You will commit more and more to always choosing a positive attitude.

Now that you have a foundation rooted in an understanding of the importance of discipline and a great attitude, there is one other part of discipline you need to master.

9

Perspective

THE "BUZZER-BEATER" IS UNQUESTIONABLY ONE OF THE most exciting moments for basketball fans. It truly is one of the most dramatic instants you will find in any sport.

For anyone reading who may not watch basketball, a buzzer-beater is when a player releases the ball completely from their hand before the clock hits zero and the buzzer sounds. As long as the shot has left the hand before the clock hits zero, it counts if it goes in.

A last-second shot when the game is tied is dramatic enough, but the tension is at its maximum if the shooting team is down by a point. In that scenario a made shot will instantly win the game, and a missed shot will lose it.

All or nothing, win or lose.

As exciting as it is, the buzzer-beater is also one of the surest ways for coaches and players (and fans for that matter) to lose perspective, which is a critical aspect of the Discipline tool. Learning to discipline yourself to see things in their proper perspective keeps you from overreacting (or sometimes underreacting) to situations.

One of the greatest sources of perspective I received in my coaching journey was from a very special couple, Les and Mary Triplett. Les won six state championships as the head boys' basketball coach at Jackson Prep in Jackson, Mississippi. He won 95 percent of the games he coached at Prep. His wife, Mary, was an outstanding basketball coach in her own right and also coached me in high school on the track team.

Les and Mary have been tremendous supporters and mentors to me for over twenty-five years. They made a point of watching the games I coached over the years, and would even tune in on the radio if the game wasn't available on television. They have just been incredible allies, for which I am so grateful.

With Les following the games I coached, he would know when we lost on a buzzer-beater or when we won on a last-second play. Being the experienced coach that he was, he knew what it felt like in these situations.

I remember one of these times in particular. Les and Mary watched us play the University of Tennessee on television. This was a game between two evenly matched teams. Both were ranked nationally in the top ten, and we were each competing hard to secure the SEC championship that season.

In this game, Tennessee was leading 60–59. But we gained possession of the ball with just a few seconds left and called time-out.

We were fortunate to have the best player in the SEC that year, A'dia Mathies. Everyone in the arena knew who the ball was going to in this situation. As we huddled during the time-out, A'dia said with great confidence to her coaches and teammates that she would make the shot.

We managed to inbound the ball to A'dia, and she drove hard to the basket. She had three Tennessee defenders trying to stop her, but it didn't matter. A'dia sliced through the defense and laid the ball into the basket before the buzzer went off.

Kentucky 61, Tennessee 60. It was a great victory for the Wildcats and was a pivotal win that ultimately led us to the 2012 SEC Championship.

After the game, we were all ecstatic, of course. And Les and Mary were super happy for us, too, but Les also shared some timely wisdom that speaks directly to perspective.

"What a great win, but let's realize something," Les said. "If A'dia missed that last shot, the score would have been 60–59. You lose by one point. This time it went in, so you won by a point. But never let a one-point win totally blind you with joy, and never let a one-point loss blind you with sadness. Always stay focused on what needs to be done to get better and help your team grow."

His point (no pun intended) was that the result of one shot could have *way* too much influence on how a coach interprets how his team played. What was particularly wise about this advice is that he gave it after we won. It's not unusual to hear things like this when you lose—people want to comfort you. But Les was reminding me that win or not, there's always more work to be done if you want to continue to grow.

Simply put, one shot should never make that much difference in how you interpret a game. Maybe your team played mostly lousy, and you were fortunate to escape with a win. Or maybe your team played fundamentally sound basketball against a great team for most of the game, and a lucky last-second shot from half-court bounced off the backboard and went in.

Perspective will allow you to better manage the emotion of winning and losing and focus on an accurate assessment of the game.

I will confess that when I was a young coach, it did not even take a buzzer-beater to make me lose perspective. I judged everything way too much through the lens of wins and losses. A win meant we played well and things must be headed in the right direction. A loss, and we had so many things we had to work on and the season was close to going down the drain. It was a very undisciplined perspective.

The world of business has very few moments that are quite as time-compressed and dramatic as a buzzer-beater. But there are happenstances every day that can cause us to allow emotions to cloud our perspective.

Maybe it is that you make a mistake and are called out on it. Suddenly, you are sure that you have damaged your career, you have blown the chance for the promotion you were hoping was coming soon, and the whole office must be looking at you as a failure.

The discipline of perspective allows a person to look at the situation in its entire context and question these assumptions. Most times, we overestimate how much others are judging us. Do a factual analysis of your mistake, do what you can to counteract it, and move forward.

Another example might be losing an important client or customer. This can obviously be serious for a business. However, spending a lot of time predicting that other clients are next and that business is about to take a severe downturn is a waste of energy. Use that energy instead to discover as precisely as possible why you lost the client. If it could have been prevented, what can you do differently with your other clients to make sure you retain them?

This is why the discipline of perspective is so important. It keeps you from overreacting and making big changes when those transformations may do more harm than good. It keeps you from wasting energy and resources while going overboard revolutionizing something that only needs minor adjustments.

On the flip side, some luck or a change in your industry may lead to a big temporary increase in sales that has everyone feeling great. But that short-term trend may only be masking bigger problems. Everyone is riding high and feeling great (like after a big win on a buzzer-beater), but under the radar are fundamental problems that need to be addressed, or trouble is ahead.

The first step toward becoming disciplined in perspective is just to recognize this very human trait of allowing the emotions of wins and losses to cloud our judgment of what is really going on. If you acknowledge it, you can work to counterbalance it. Almost nothing is ever as good as we think it is right after a big win, a big promotion, or a big sale. And almost nothing is ever as bad as we think it is after a huge loss or setback.

Recalling this in the moment is half the battle in bringing the discipline of perspective to the table.

Perspective

PERSPECTIVE WHEN INTERACTING WITH OTHERS

A key to the discipline of perspective is how we interact with others. We need other viewpoints and honest feedback to keep our assessments on target. The problem comes in when we have a preconceived idea of what a person is going to tell us.

We hear what we expect to hear, instead of listening for what a person is trying to communicate to us. You also have to remember that someone may be struggling to communicate what they mean. Not everyone you work with is going to be a polished communicator.

The solution is to listen and ask questions about what you are hearing. Repeat things back for understanding. This forces you to make the shift from hearing what you expected to actively searching for what the other person wants to communicate.

I think the danger of miscommunication is also greatly increased by the tools we use to communicate now. So much of our human-to-human interaction has become filtered through digital devices. Like everyone, I use text messages and emails a lot. There are so many good things about it, especially for quick messages conveying straightforward information.

However, there is a downside when communicating more subtle things, like emotions or working through a problem or communicating a needed change. I have had it happen where I receive a text message from someone, and it sends up a red flag

139

for me that something terrible is going on. Then I call them and find out I had way overinterpreted what was said, and everything is pretty much fine.

As part of the discipline of perspective, we need to remember that digital communication has some serious weaknesses because it is much harder to convey tone. You cannot tell how fast or slow a person is talking; there are no body language cues—you just lose so much. Of course, this is not a plea to eliminate digital communications. But I do think the more we can actually talk to people by phone, or even better, face to face, the more accurate perspective we will have.

NEGATIVE SELF-TALK IS A HUGE PERSPECTIVE KILLER

Maybe it is just because I struggled with it so much in my own personal journey, but I think the number one killer of the discipline of perspective is negative self-talk.

I will tell you that one of the places I still struggle with it is when I golf. I am sure many of you who play the game will be able to relate to this, but even if you don't, I think you will get what I am saying. Before my game begins, I go in thinking about how I will shoot par that day.

For those that do not golf, par is the number of shots it should take you to get the ball in the cup on any particular hole (assuming you play it well). So I am hopeful. Then the first two holes start off with a couple of double bogeys (a double bogey is taking two shots above par to get the ball in the hole). I am growing frustrated but am still hopeful that I can recover and get within shouting distance of par.

Then I send my first shot on the third hole out of bounds. That will require a penalty stroke, and you can pretty much forget about par on this hole too. Now I begin to really beat myself up, and the soundtrack in my head becomes, *You are the worst golfer in the world.*

I have totally lost perspective, and because of that, my game is likely to keep getting worse that day. Being that I am not a professional golfer, this, of course, will not be disastrous. But it is a bad habit to let negative self-talk become a regular thing in any area of your life.

In other areas, negative self-talk can be a huge problem. It can stop us from believing we can succeed, and it creates a destructive feedback loop.

In the Honesty section of the book, I emphasized not sugar-coating the truth, especially to ourselves. So where do you draw the line between honest self-assessment and negative self-talk?

First, ask yourself in any self-critique, "Am I dealing with facts here, or am I dealing with emotions?" If you are emphasizing factual, reality-based problems, then you are on the right track. If your internal voice is simply haranguing you with name-calling and emotional diatribes, that means you have lost perspective.

Another way to tell the difference between honesty and negativity is to check in with others who you trust. Ask them to help you get a true perspective on the problem you are addressing. No matter how good we get at this discipline, no one can have perfect perspective on themselves. Use others to give you a wide enough lens to see yourself accurately.

It can even be helpful if these mentors, loved ones, coworkers, and friends we rely on for perspective are the kind that will let you vent a little first. We are human, and sometimes verbalizing all the negativity and blame and unhelpful junk in our heads lets us clear it (as long as we don't take it too far and go on endlessly). The best people in your life will listen and then help redirect you back to the facts.

OLD-SCHOOL COACHING

Coaching not that long ago was different than it is today. While there is much to admire and appreciate in the "old-school" approach, I think it is time to admit that it also had some drawbacks.

I learned those ways growing up and put into practice many old-school techniques. And I carried them for far too long in my own coaching, thinking that it was effective. One of the reasons I am writing this book is I want to share these ideas with any business leader today who may still think that sarcasm or fear is an effective motivation strategy. I am not saying it never works; I am simply saying that it is not very effective nor will it be an enduring leadership model. People will either tune you out or leave.

When I was a young person, it was considered perfectly acceptable and even good coaching to motivate players through fear. This certainly was not the only technique used by coaches, but striking fear in the hearts of the team was definitely considered one of the motivational tools available in the coaching toolbox.

I carried this with me in my own career. I would use sarcasm if I thought it would help reinforce a point. As I shared earlier in the book, I had to have a reckoning with how my anger played into all these coaching "strategies." Working through that helped me think through other things I was doing.

For example, at one point in my career, when I was observing a player doing something incorrectly, I would stop them and ask them sharply, "What are you doing?" or "What's wrong with you? Haven't we been over this?" Of course, I was not asking them these questions because I really wanted an answer. I knew perfectly well what they were doing because I was watching them. This was just a harsh and unhelpful way to call them out on it.

I eventually learned to stop asking questions of this type. I learned to listen more to what players were saying. If I did see something that needed correction, I abandoned sarcastic comments and would tell them accurately and specifically what they needed to do instead.

For instance, I would say something like, "I need you to do a better job of securing a rebound by using two hands, not one." Or "I need you to play with more balanced feet." I am still pointing out that there must be improvement, but I am doing it in a concrete way that gives them something specific to work on.

If you are a bit of an old-school leader yourself, you might be thinking, *Okay, I see what you are saying, but sometimes you do need to be very direct. Having some fear that you will be called out and embarrassed does have motivational value.*

I'm not saying you can't be direct; as I have said previously in the book, I do not think sugarcoating helps anyone get better, and it hurts the team overall. I am saying you can get your point across without going over the line into bullying, sarcasm, cursing, or humiliation.

Building on the example above, I might say to a player, "I need you to rebound with two hands, not one." And then if I wanted to emphasize it, I would say in a very direct way, "And I need that done starting immediately." Communicating like this gets your point across in a motivating way, but without sarcasm or humiliation.

Of course, you will want to adjust how exactly you deliver messages and in what tone based on the specifics of your workplace situation and within the acceptable range of modern workplace standards. The point is to think about how you are coming across, how effective it is, and whether you are disciplining what you are saying and how you are saying it with the necessary perspective.

I received good counsel on perspective beginning at a very young age from my mom. My dad could be a bit intense, and that carried over to my brothers and me, but my mother was a great and wise counterbalance in the family.

In fact, when it comes to disciplined perspective, she is one of the best practitioners I've ever encountered. I remember her telling my brothers and me quite often that "sarcasm comes from the Greek word *sarkasmos*, which means 'the tearing of flesh.' You can't help anyone move forward when you are tearing their flesh."

And she did not just counsel against negative words, valuable as that was. She also had a philosophy that was perfectly encapsulated in one of her favorite pieces of advice: "Wear life like a loose-fitting garment."

This was her way of telling us to just keep giving our best, and don't stress out when things didn't go our way. All you have to do is keep wearing life a little loosely, continue to do your best, and you *will* eventually succeed.

If you wear life a little too intensely, it can become all too easy to descend into negativity and lash out at people with sarcasm or intimidation. Later in life, as I made changes to myself, her words served as a guide. They helped me make the shift from an old-school coaching mentality to an approach that had much clearer and more productive communication.

I hope nothing I am saying here is giving someone the impression that leaders should not be stringent in holding people accountable. That would fly in the face of so many other things I have advocated in this book.

Here's another example to show you what I mean. A common consequence a basketball coach would give for infractions or laziness in practice is to line the team up for wind sprints. Like you would guess from the name, these are not fun. You end up huffing and puffing, and they are boring compared to playing basketball.

The team needs to know what will trigger wind sprints, and you must make them do them if their actions warrant it. I have known some leaders and coaches who think you can catch more flies with honey than vinegar. We all have different styles, but no matter your style, I think consistent consequences are necessary for success.

To sum up this example, an old-school coach might get angry about how practice is going and blurt out, "Line up, we're doing thirty wind sprints!" (That typically would be considered a harsh, ridiculous amount.) The more often these overly severe punishments happen, the more your team catches on that you are just being an arbitrary tyrant who is basing the "consequences" on your mood.

A "too nice" coach might see that the team is not putting in their best effort, but thinks, *Not today. Players are bound to have off days sometimes, so why make them hate me by making them do wind sprints?*

Excellent coaches and leaders see a problem and then give consistent consequences based on an accurate assessment. "I said the next time someone went up for a rebound without both hands, the entire team would run two wind sprints. Line up."

If you are currently managing people at work, this is how you need to discipline your own thinking and emotions. Are you coming down on your team arbitrarily because someone above you in the hierarchy did the same to you, and now you're mad? Do you know a team member needs a coaching memo that will be hard to deliver, so you avoid it because you do not want to risk being disliked?

Or are you honestly assessing people based on what you see and the facts and then delivering the consequences fairly and professionally? These are important questions to think through if you want to reach the highest levels of leadership.

PRAISING NEGATIVE OUTCOMES

It sounds a little crazy at first, but the discipline of perspective means you need to sometimes single out a bad outcome for praise.

For example, I sometimes made it a point to praise turnovers made by players. Earlier in the book, we talked about the importance of turnover margin. An overall high turnover rate is a sign of a team with problems on offense, and individual turnovers are often the result of sloppy play.

However, that does not mean that *every* turnover is a bad play. Sometimes a turnover happens because a player took a proper risk to make a good play, and the other team made a spectacular defensive play to stop it. If I would get upset about a turnover like that, the message I would be sending my team is "don't ever take risks" and "it doesn't matter that you were playing the game the right way, if it goes wrong, you are going to get negative feedback."

A good leader will not criticize someone for doing the right thing but getting a bad result. A great leader will actually praise a right action even though it did not work out that particular time.

When you praise the right action despite the result, you are reinforcing that you are the kind of leader who has mastered the discipline of perspective. You take the time to honestly evaluate situations, instead of just blurting out knee-jerk reactions.

Having the discipline of perspective allows you to analyze situations like this appropriately. Instead of "You lost that sale, that means you must have made a mistake," you can analyze it and realize, "You lost that sale because you would not give the customer the unreasonable concessions they demanded to go through with it. You did the right thing."

MORE EMOTIONALLY HEALTHY

If you are a leader who grew up around the time I did, you may feel that taking time to work on your own emotions with the help of others is a sign of weakness. You may think it will mark you out as someone who does not have top leadership qualities.

I now think the opposite. Having the courage to work on yourself makes you a stronger, more empathetic leader. This is not guesswork on my part; it is my direct experience talking.

I have used counselors a few times in my life, and each time I've engaged, I've learned more about how to more effectively manage my emotions. For me, it has been life-changing. By taking this risk to change and develop a higher emotional intelligence, I became a much better leader.

The older model of a leader as someone who equates admitting needing help with being a sign of weakness is outdated. The best leaders know they are best prepared to lead when they work on their own emotional health.

IT'S TIME TO BRING IT ALL TOGETHER

You now hold the keys to character-based leadership that can power your success for a lifetime. You need Honesty to keep you in touch with reality and know if you are truly heading in the right direction; you need Hard Work because greatness never happens without it; and you need Discipline to be the glue that holds it all together. Let's bring this all together now into a concise summary, so you can get started using the Winning Tools.

Conclusion

As of this writing, I've been practicing yoga for over two years. My yoga instructor, Kate Kaiser, is one of the most positive people in my life. Each time we practice, we go through a couple of different sequences in the first two-thirds of the session. As we get to our final sequence, Kate always says, "Let's put this all together."

It's her way of reminding me to take all of the best movements of our practice and combine them to finish our practice strong. That's the spirit I bring to this Conclusion section: let's put this all together and finish strong!

I want to leave you with five key takeaways to remember if you want to get the most out of the Winning Tools as you go on your leadership journey.

Key Takeaway #1: Simple Does Not Mean Easy

After decades of coaching and leadership, I now know that a commitment to simple, fundamental principles is the key to a purposeful life. I also find that many people miss this because they think, "Oh, that advice is too simple."

The truth is that the best tools and concepts usually *are* simple. But simple is not the same as easy. My hope is that you will use the examples, stories, and principles in this book to deeply reflect on the Winning Tools and commit to implementing them. You will see how powerful they are when you don't dismiss them as "too simple."

Key Takeaway #2: Principles Over Emotion

The Winning Tools work because they make you a principled-driven thinker as opposed to an emotion-driven thinker. Our emotions will fluctuate from day to day, hour to hour, and even minute to minute. We have incredible highs and devastating lows, with everything else in between.

That kind of fluctuation means emotion-driven thinking is unreliable. When we commit to the principles of Honesty, Hard Work, and Discipline, we can think our way through the challenges of life with reliability and consistency.

Key Takeaway #3: Be Rigorously Honest

Honesty can be a big topic with a lot of different aspects, including temptations like self-deception and not wanting to hurt the feelings of others.

At heart, though, it is not that complicated. Don't just be surface honest. Don't think, *Well, technically I didn't lie.* Don't shrug off the criticism of people you respect because it hurts to think about your shortcomings.

Forget all the excuses and just commit to being rigorously honest. Do it starting now, and keep working at this. It is both a commitment and a skill. Try rigorous honesty as an experiment for a year if you doubt me. You will love the results.

Key Takeaway #4: Hard Work is Nonnegotiable

Everyone loves a hack or a shortcut. And maybe sometimes there are a few of these that can help you for small things.

I guarantee you, however, that there are no shortcuts if you want genuine life accomplishments. You can't skip the work, period. For a life that is purposeful and earns you respect and success, hard work is absolutely nonnegotiable.

Forget magic pills, and the cavalry won't be coming either. If you want to accomplish great things and lead others to do the same, you will have to work extremely hard.

Key Takeaway #5: Discipline is the Glue that Holds the Tools Together

People who burn to earn leadership positions sometimes struggle with this tool. When you want to be your best, it sometimes feels like success can't come fast enough. And perspective is hard when you are tempted to perfectionism.

I know these problems all too well! It's why I'm such a firm believer in continuing to hone the skills of discipline. Honesty and hard work will take you only part of the journey. You will lose your way without discipline.

Discipline is the final piece of the puzzle, the one that separates the good from the great. Work hard on making discipline a lifelong habit, and you will reap rewards far greater than you ever could otherwise.

There's one last thing I'd like to share. It is one last takeaway for the book, and a way to honor three special people who helped me sharpen my own Winning Tools.

Throughout this book I hope you noticed how many times I mentioned the people who have mentored and supported me. This is not an accident, and it is not puffery. If you want to be a successful leader, you need all kinds of supporters, mentors, and loving family and friends.

I think sometimes there's this notion that the best in their fields are "lone wolf" types who through their own strength and grit lift themselves to awesome heights above everyone else. Strength, grit, and self-direction are all good and necessary qualities. But they are not enough. I will take a relationship builder over a lone wolf any day.

So here is one last takeaway: to get the most out of the Winning Tools, find and cultivate relationships with people who already model these tools in real life. Learn to spot Honesty, Hard Work, and Discipline in others and learn from them. Here are three models from my own life.

The Honesty of Mitch Barnhart

Mitch Barnhart, the Kentucky athletic director, hired me and gave me the opportunity of a lifetime. Mitch is one of the most dynamic leaders I've ever encountered. What he has built at Kentucky during his tenure is remarkable. And the foundation of it all is that he is without a doubt one of the most honest leaders I know.

The Hard Work of Mickie DeMoss

Coach DeMoss was my predecessor at Kentucky and one of the greatest mentors I've ever had. I worked for Mickie at Kentucky as an assistant for two years before I became a head coach. I never worked for or with anyone who worked as hard as Mickie. She taught me the value of doing a job fully, with precision, and with efficiency. I transformed into an effective hard worker through her guidance and example.

The Discipline of Jenna Mitchell

My wife, Jenna, is the most disciplined leader I know. During my time at Kentucky, I never made a major decision without her counsel. Jenna is a master of keeping perspective and never allowed me to wallow in negative self-talk, and she unfailingly encouraged me to believe in myself as a coach. *I* didn't win 333 Division I college basketball games. *Jenna and I* did that together, with her discipline and perspective inspiring me.

So lastly, I encourage you to never forget that if you want to be a purposeful, respected, and successful leader, you'll never get there alone. Seek out your own honest Mitch, your own hard-working Mickie, and your own disciplined Jenna, whatever their actual names turn out to be.

With the right examples and the right principles, you'll become a master of the Winning Tools and unlock the life you deserve.

Acknowledgments

I WANT TO THANK THE FOLLOWING PEOPLE FOR INVESTing in my coaching journey:

To Mark and Mary Shapley, you both saw potential and encouraged me to go find a purpose. What a selfless gift you gave!

To Coach Rigby, you were there when I needed you to point me in the direction of purpose. Thank you!

To Les and Mary Triplett, you both were there for me from the very beginning and have never left my side. Your wisdom, support, and encouragement along the way sustained and enhanced my development. Thank you!

To Kim Rosamond, the positive impact you've had on my life and career cannot be overstated. You encouraged and supported me from the start of my career and have continued that through all these years. I am so very grateful for the opportunities you provided. Your friendship is treasured!

To Jan Sojourner, Bobby West, Sharon Fanning, Mark Hudspeth, Dan Boice, Durwin Carpenter, and Billy Jack Caston: you all invested significant time in the early stages of my career. I never forgot the lessons learned from each one of you. Thank you for the generosity of time and your encouragement.

To all of the players I had the opportunity to coach at Winston Academy, Central Holmes Christian School, Manchester Academy, the University of Tennessee, the University of Florida, Morehead State University, and the University of Kentucky: I am confident I learned more from you than you learned from me. I appreciate all of the effort you gave.

To Pat Summitt, Carol Ross, Carolyn Peck, Lin Dunn, and Mickie DeMoss: the lessons I learned from you helped prepare me to lead a college basketball program. I am indebted.

To Dr. Wayne Andrews and Brian Hutchinson, you both gave me an opportunity to lead my first college basketball program at Morehead State University. What an incredible experience! Thank you!

To Dr. Lee Todd, Dr. Eli Capilouto, and Mitch Barnhart: coaching at Kentucky changed the trajectory of my life immensely for the better. I am extremely grateful.

Acknowledgments

To Coach Rich Brooks, thank you for encouraging me and showing me the value of wise counsel. Your wisdom, confidence, and encouragement meant the world to me as I got started at Kentucky. Many thanks!

To John Calipari, you supported us and shined a spotlight on our program that made a difference. You did it when you didn't have to, and I will always appreciate that. Thank you!

To Kyra Elzy, we were a great team, and we did great work together. You made me better. Thank you!

To Amy Tilley, I never worked with anyone more loyal and encouraging. Thank you for your belief.

To Susan Lax, we met on the very first day I arrived at the University of Kentucky. It is a friendship that has endured all of these years, and I have great respect for the person and professional you are.

To the team at Scribe Media, Mikey Kershisnik, Renee Malove, and Michael Nagin: this was an awesome team that made this an awesome journey. I can't wait for our next one!

To the Winning Tools team, Megan Wojcik, Jess Stack, Courtney Spain, and Larry Hubatka: thanks for all of your hard work that helps us soar!

To Ted Butler, the friendship and support you've given through Operation Athlete have strengthened my mind, body, and spirit in a significant way. I am grateful for you, Brother!

To Kate Kaiser, thank you for giving me the gift of more functional movement and modeling a kind, caring, and resilient attitude. I am grateful!

To David Moffitt, you are an incredible writer, and thank you for helping bring my thoughts to life. Let's write ten more books together!

To Tom Nerney, you taught me how to think differently which led to much success. You are one of the most influential people I ever met. I thank God for putting you in my path. Thank you!

To Forrest Larson, I learned a lot about the kind of coach I wanted to be from you. Thank you for the contribution you made to my life as a coach, a teacher, and a leader.

To Tom Ostrom, your friendship, love, and support for over twenty years has impacted my life immeasurably. You are a true brother! Thank you for all you've done for me!

To John Maxwell, you changed my life forever, even before I met you! Your friendship, mentorship, and example of a faith-filled existence elevate my life. Thank you!

Acknowledgments

To my parents, John and Carol: I received a great gift from you two being my parents. You are the greatest role models I could have ever had. Thank you for teaching me the importance of the Winning Tools and the importance of faith in God. I love you!

To my brothers, David, Mark, and Stephen: your love and support through the years was motivating and greatly appreciated. Best brothers ever! Much love to you three!

To my daughter, Lacy: thank you for believing I had something worth saying. You got this whole ball rolling! I love you, and I am proud of you!

To my daughters, Saylor and Presley: I love watching you both grow. You have gifts that the world will benefit from. I love you both, and I am proud of you!

To my wife, Jenna, you have given me so much love and support in the past, and you continue to encourage my growth as a husband, father, friend, and leader. You make me better in every way, and I thank God for you every day! I love you!

To God Almighty and His Son, Jesus Christ. I am redeemed! Thank you!

About the Author

Leadership coach, mentor, and speaker Matthew Mitchell is a three-time SEC Coach of the Year and the winningest head coach in the history of the University of Kentucky women's basketball program. He established the Winning Tools principles as the foundation for his teams' success. Mitchell's focus on the fundamentals led to seven twenty-five-plus winning seasons and UK's first SEC Championship in thirty years.

Mitchell now helms the Winning Tools leadership platform, sharing the proven value of these principles to high-level leaders and teams. He and his wife Jenna founded the Mitchell Family Foundation, a nonprofit organization that benefits Lexington charities.